Mandalas for Meditaion
by Morgan Imhoff

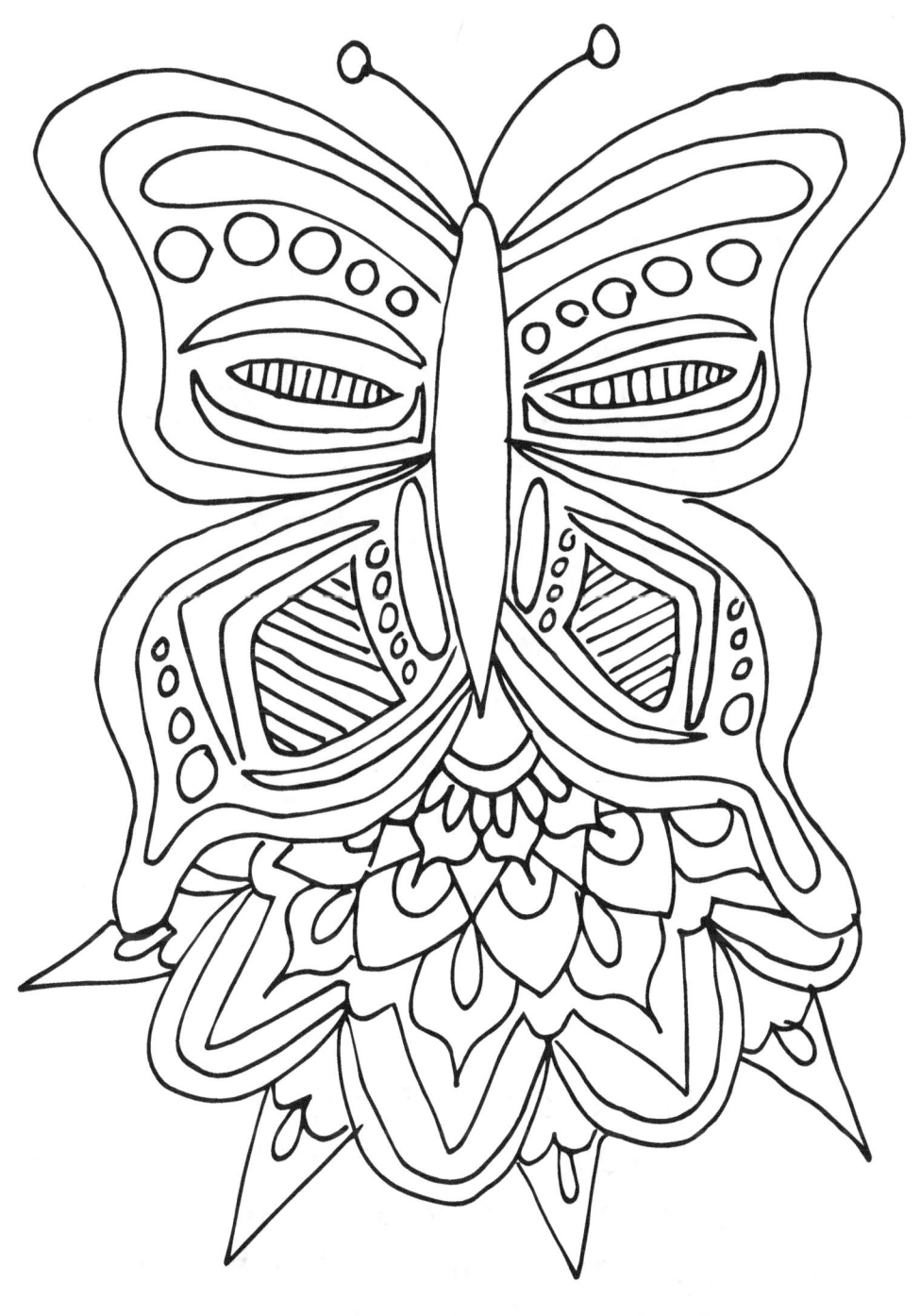

Copyright © 2017 by Morgan Imhoff
All rights reserved. No part of this book may be
reproduced in any form without
writen permission from the publisher.
produced by createspace
ISBN 13978-1979773867

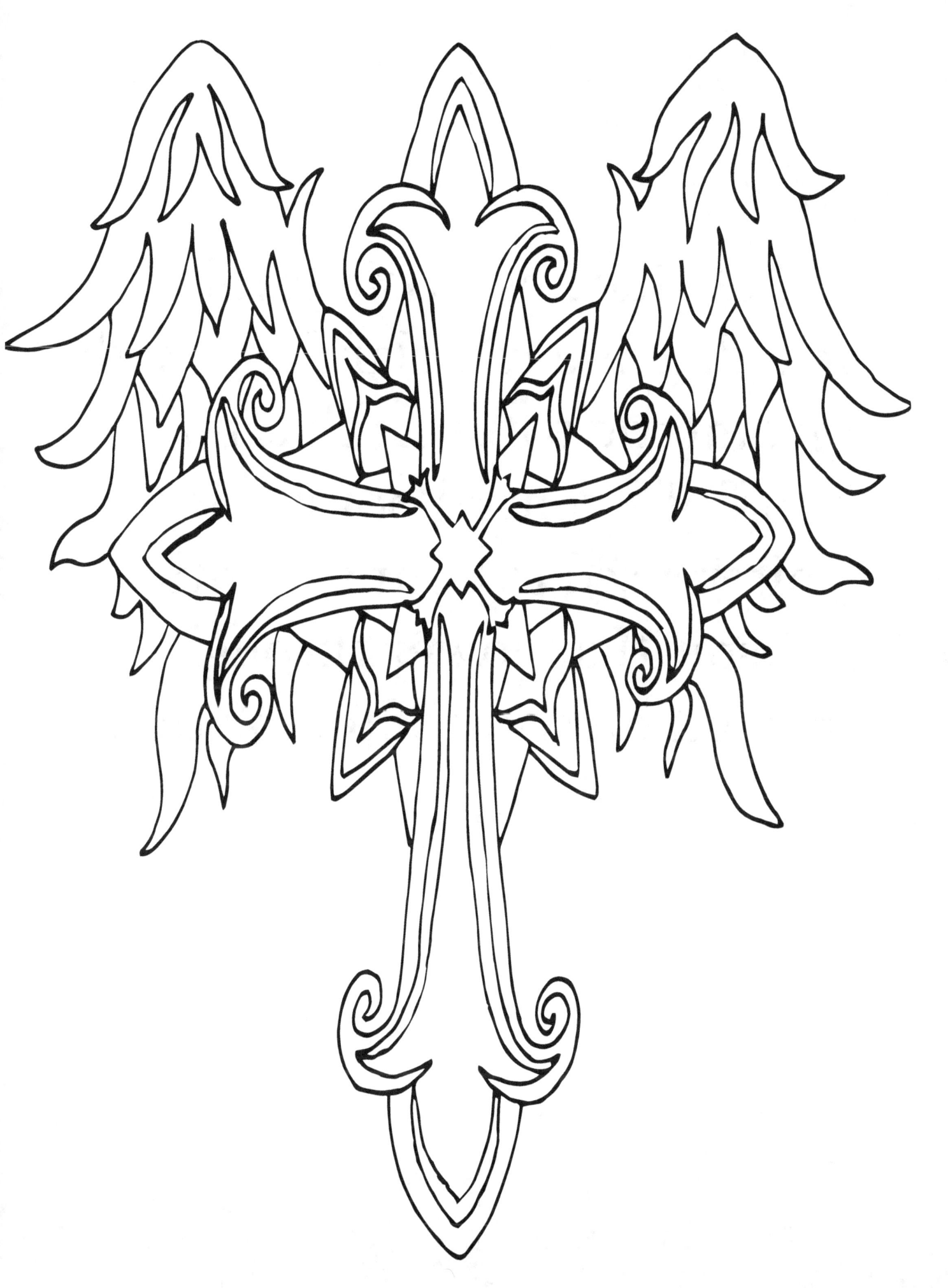

"On its most basic level, a mandala is a circular form with geometric patterns that builds off of a central point, most often used to connect with a spiritual power through meditation and contemplation."

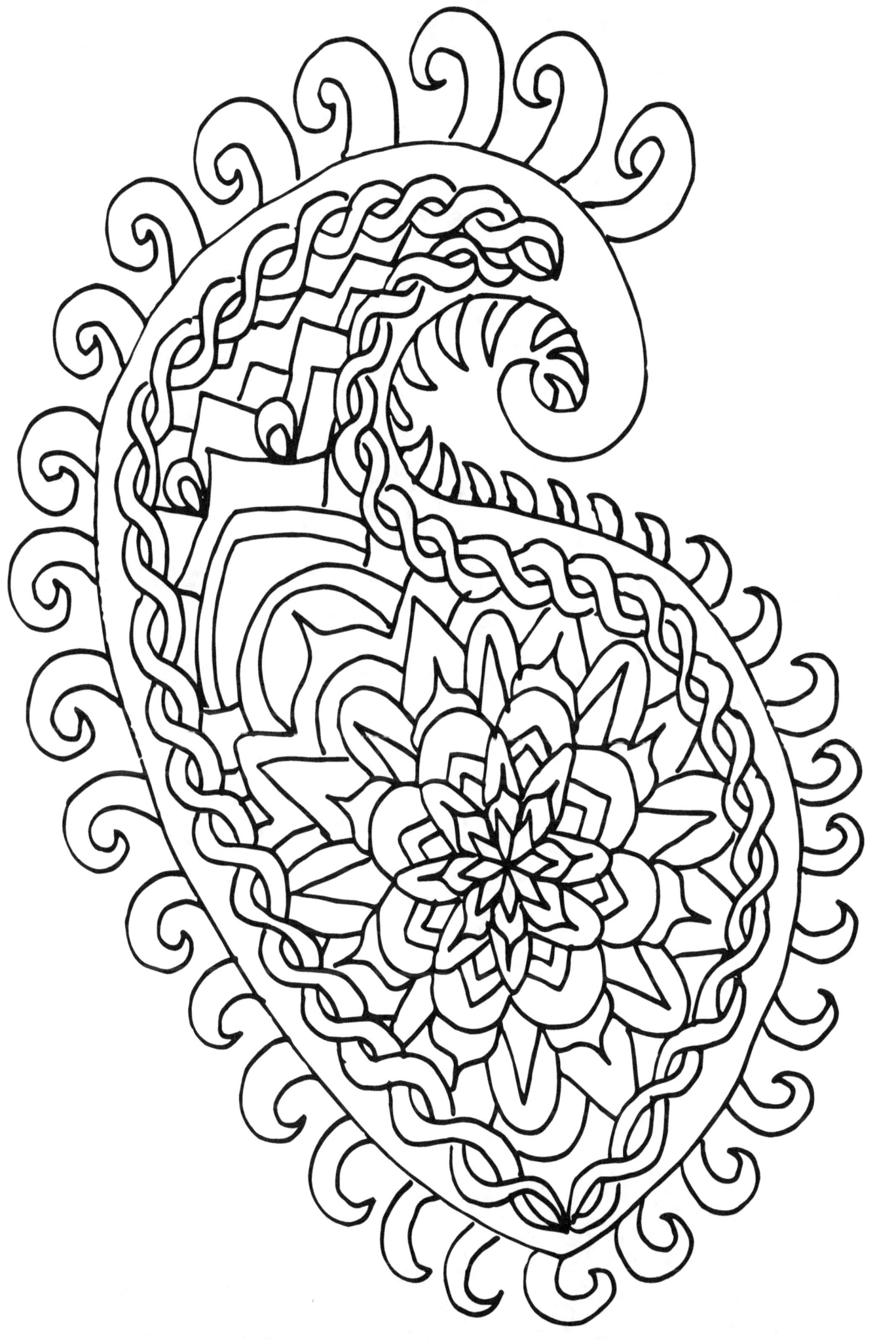

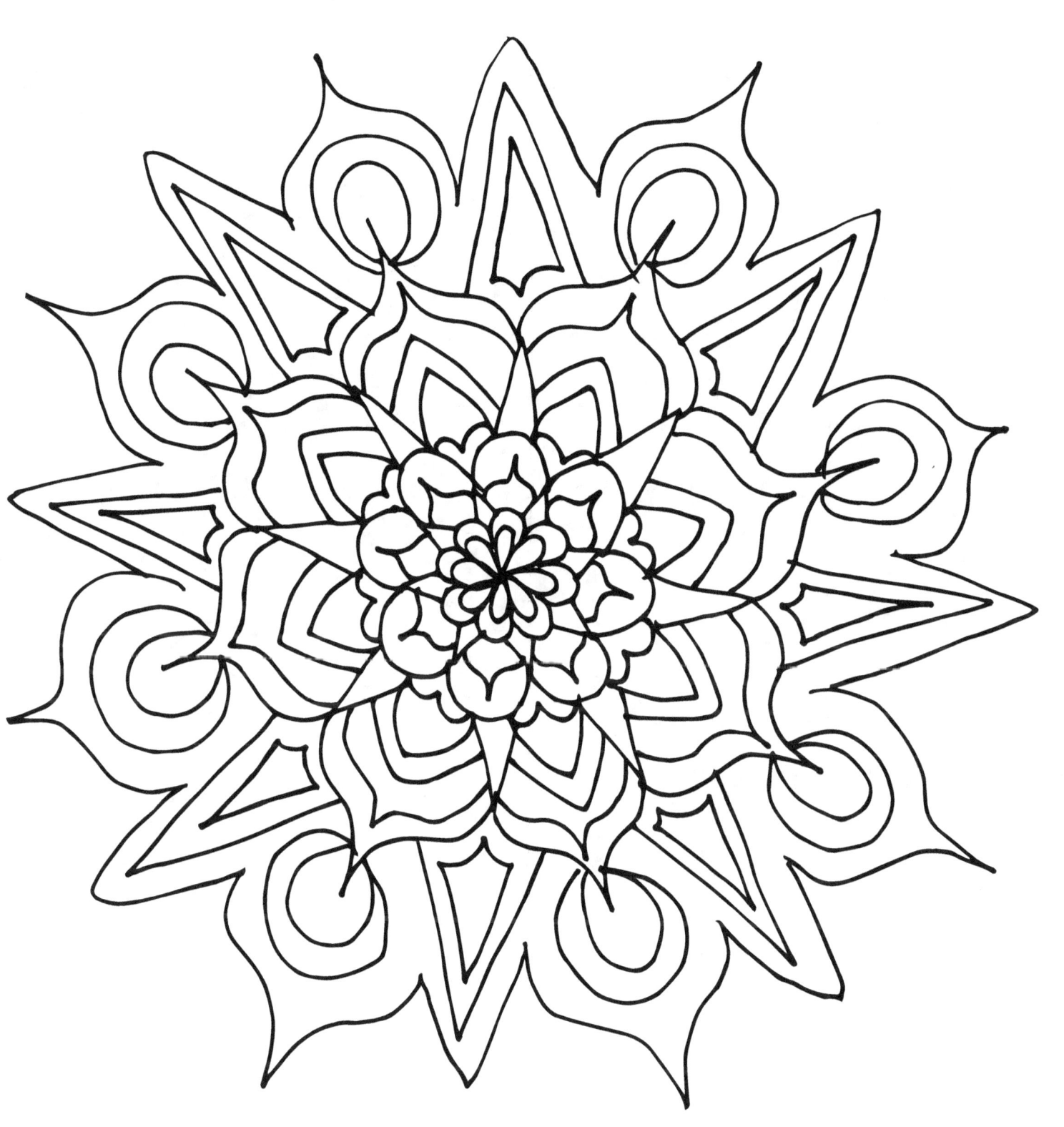

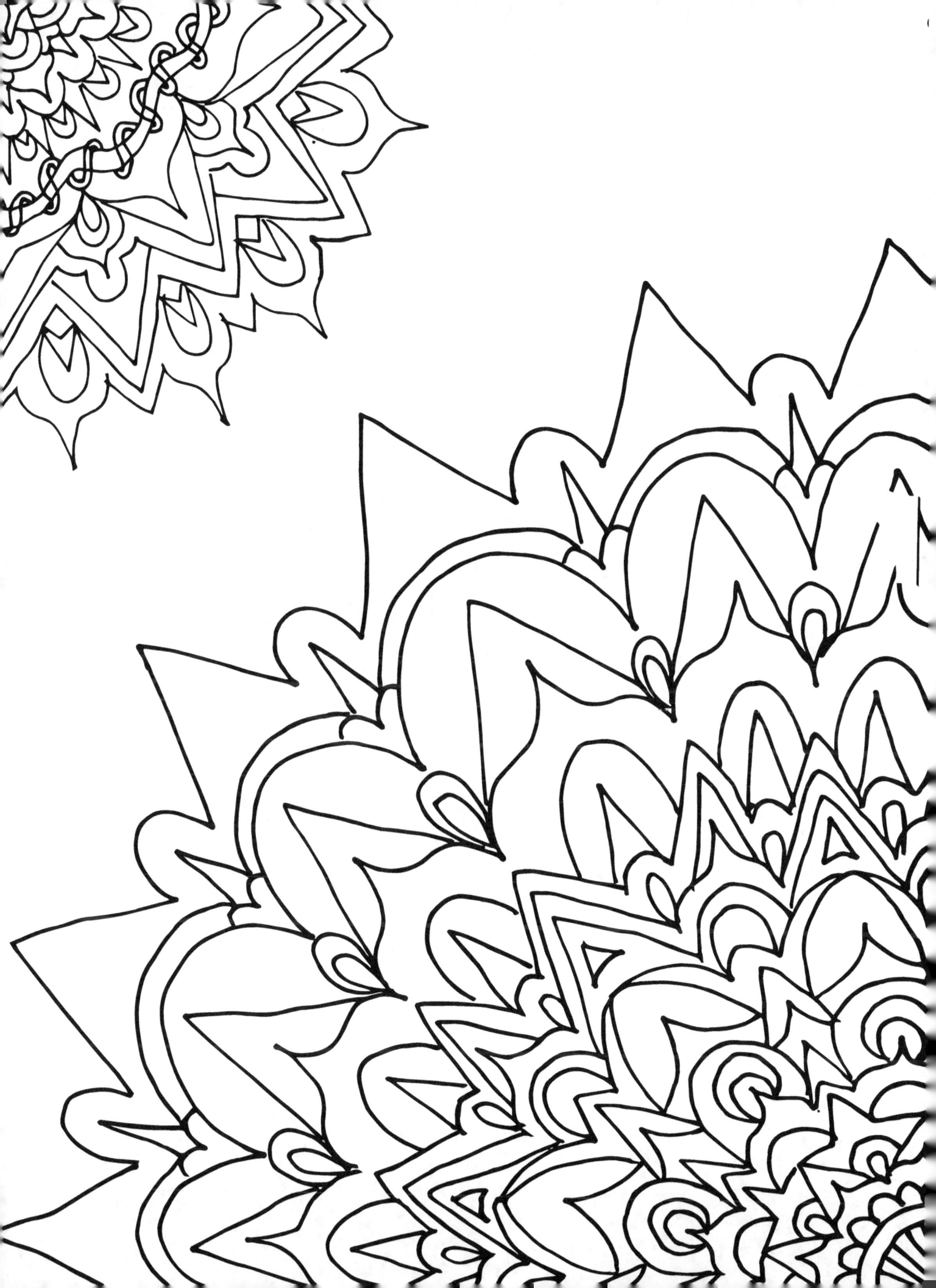

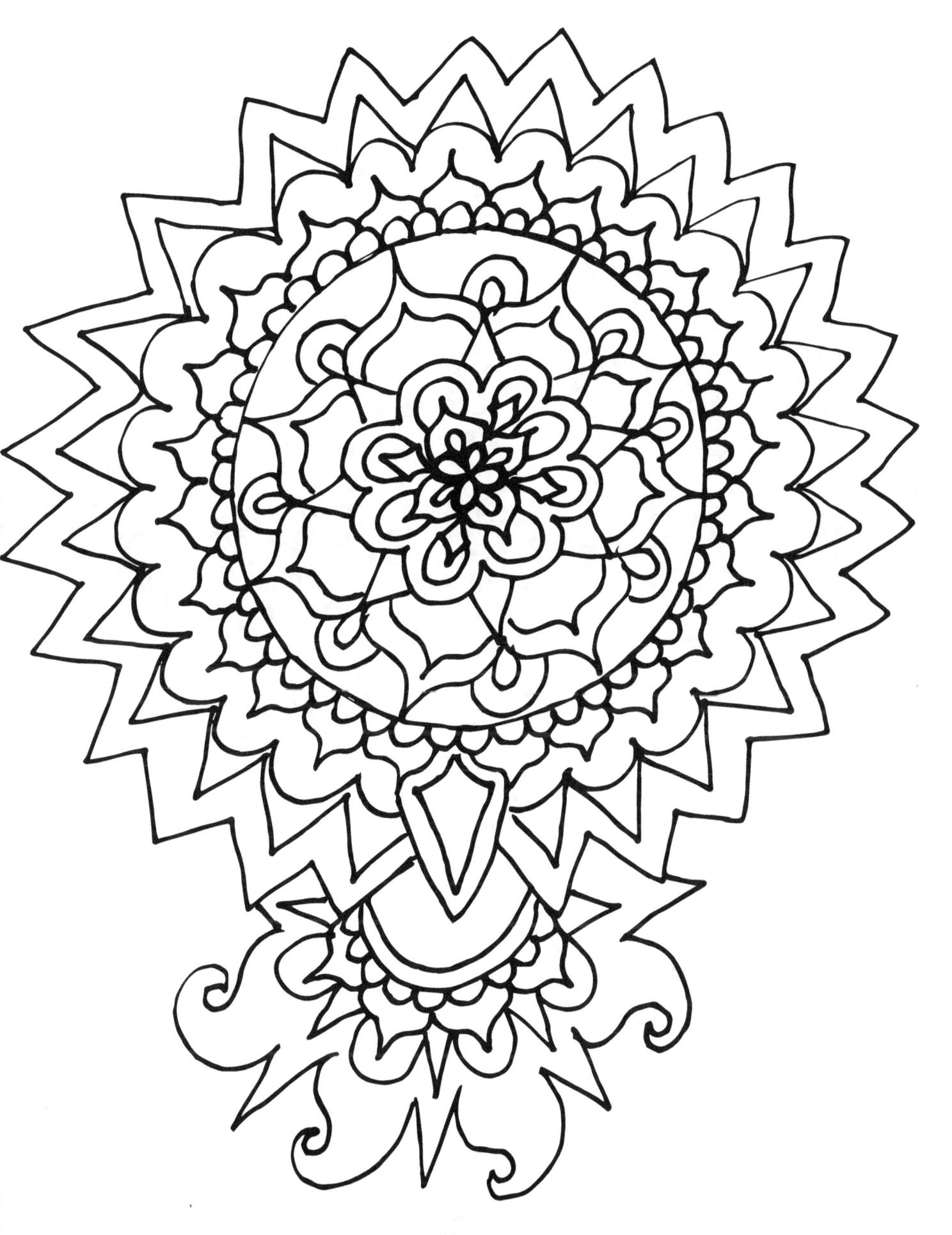

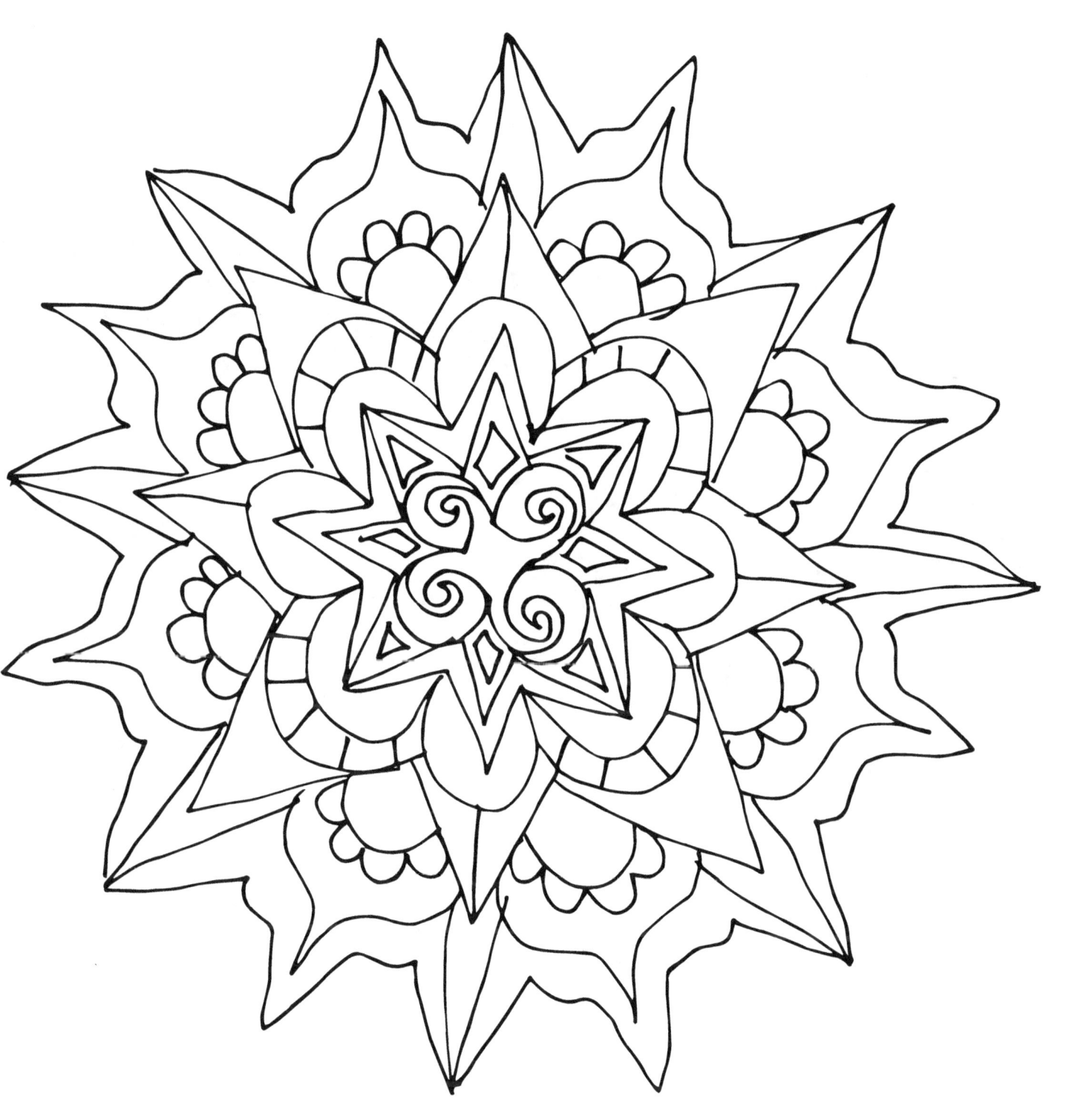

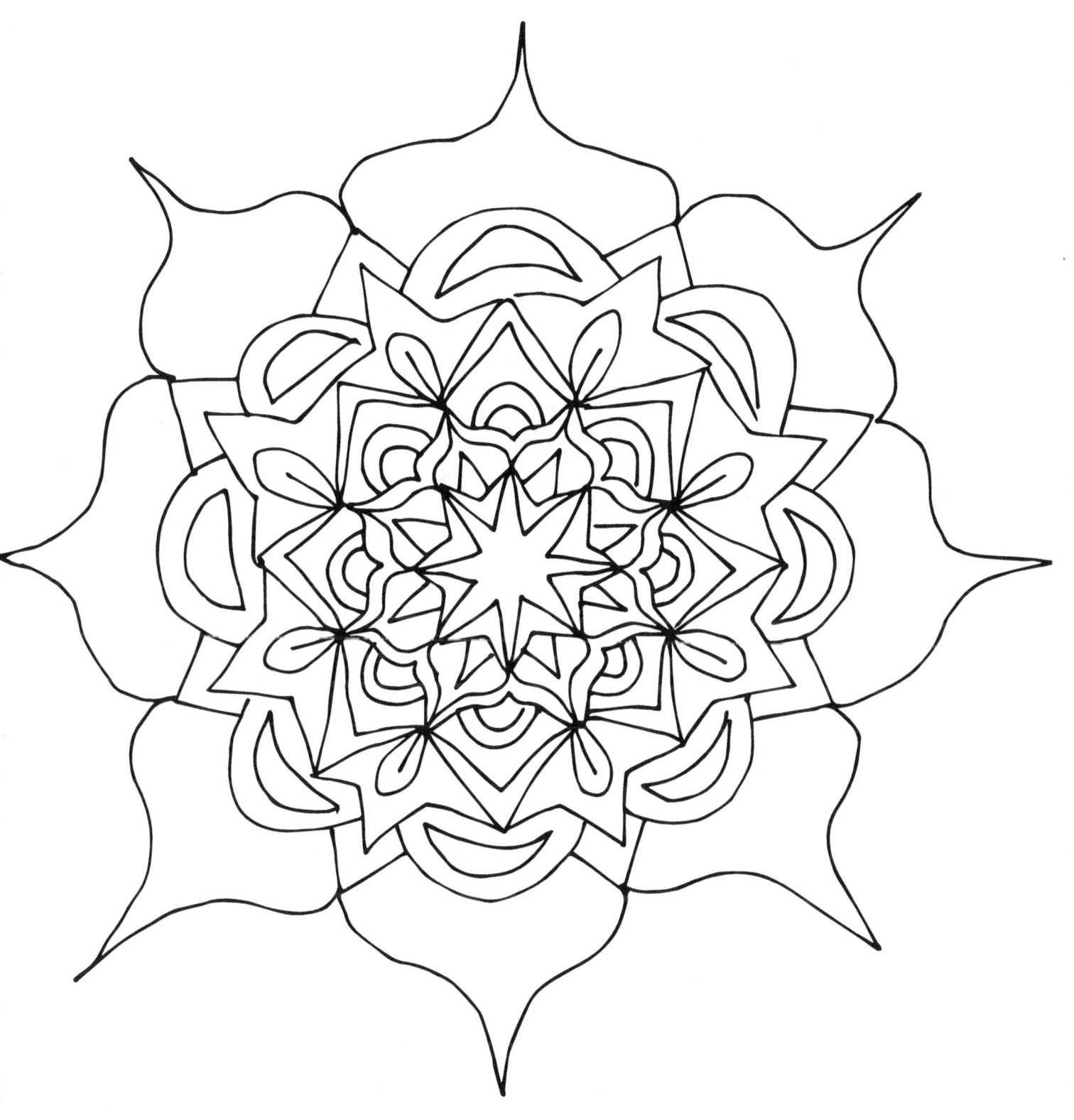

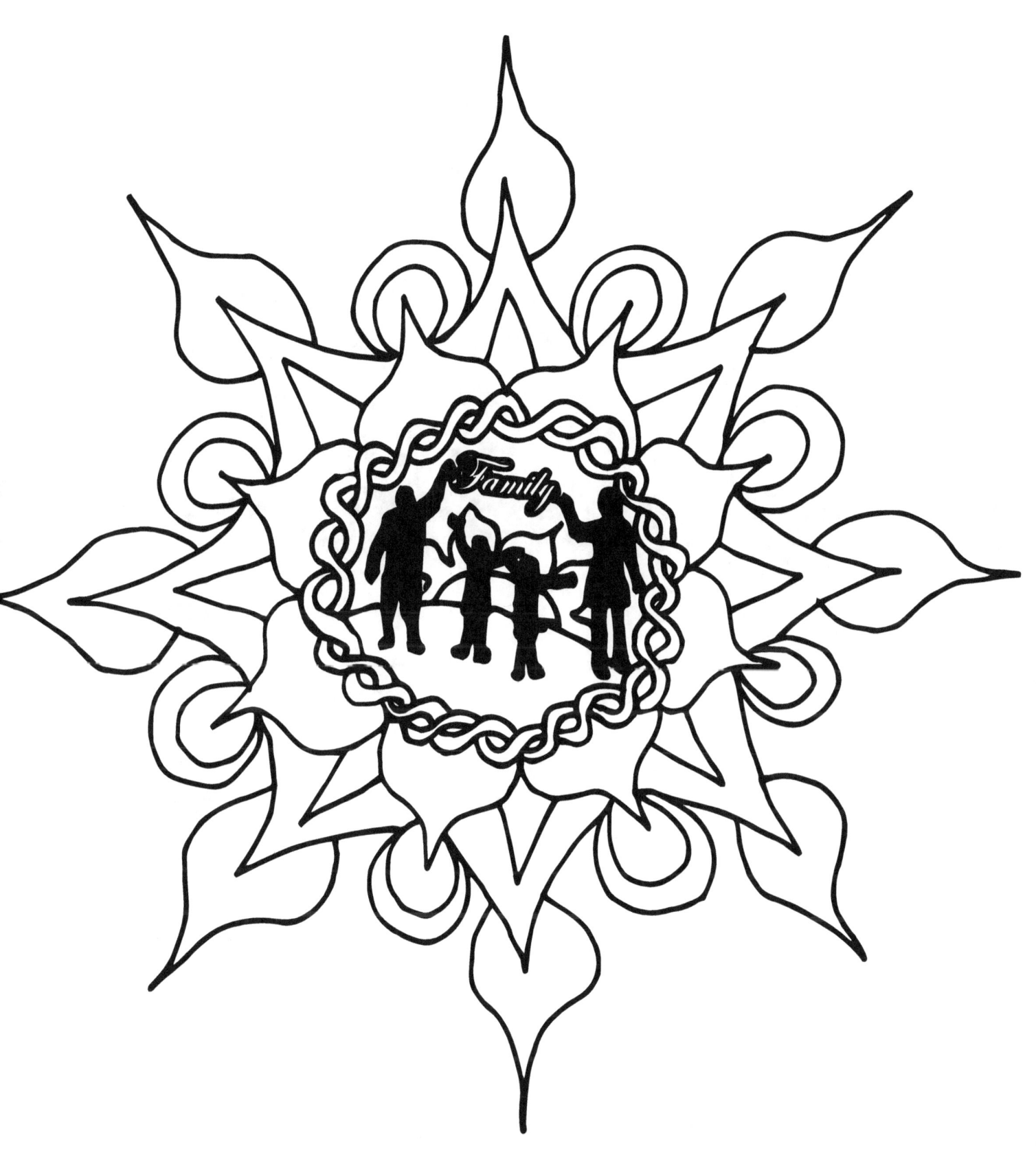

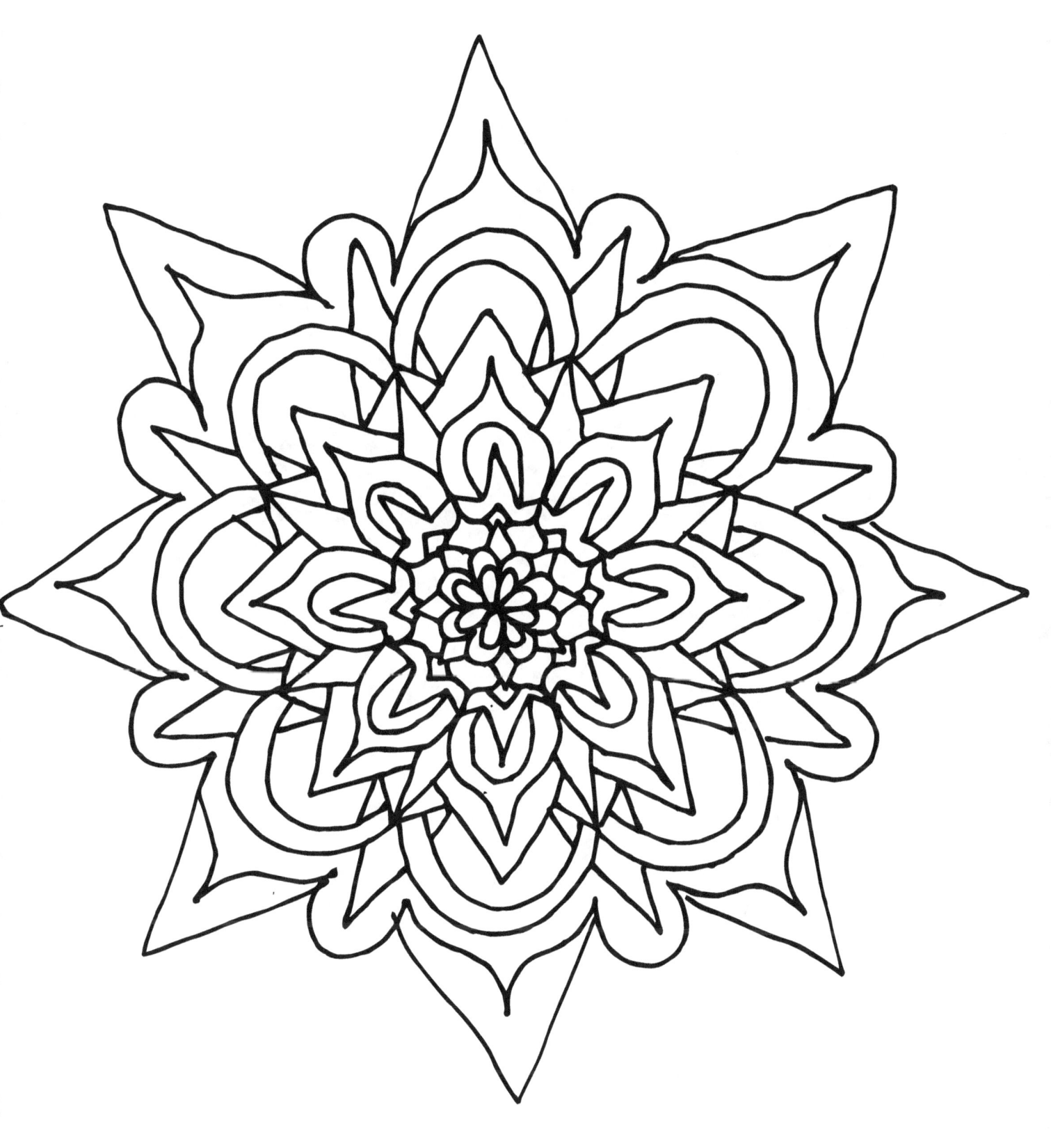

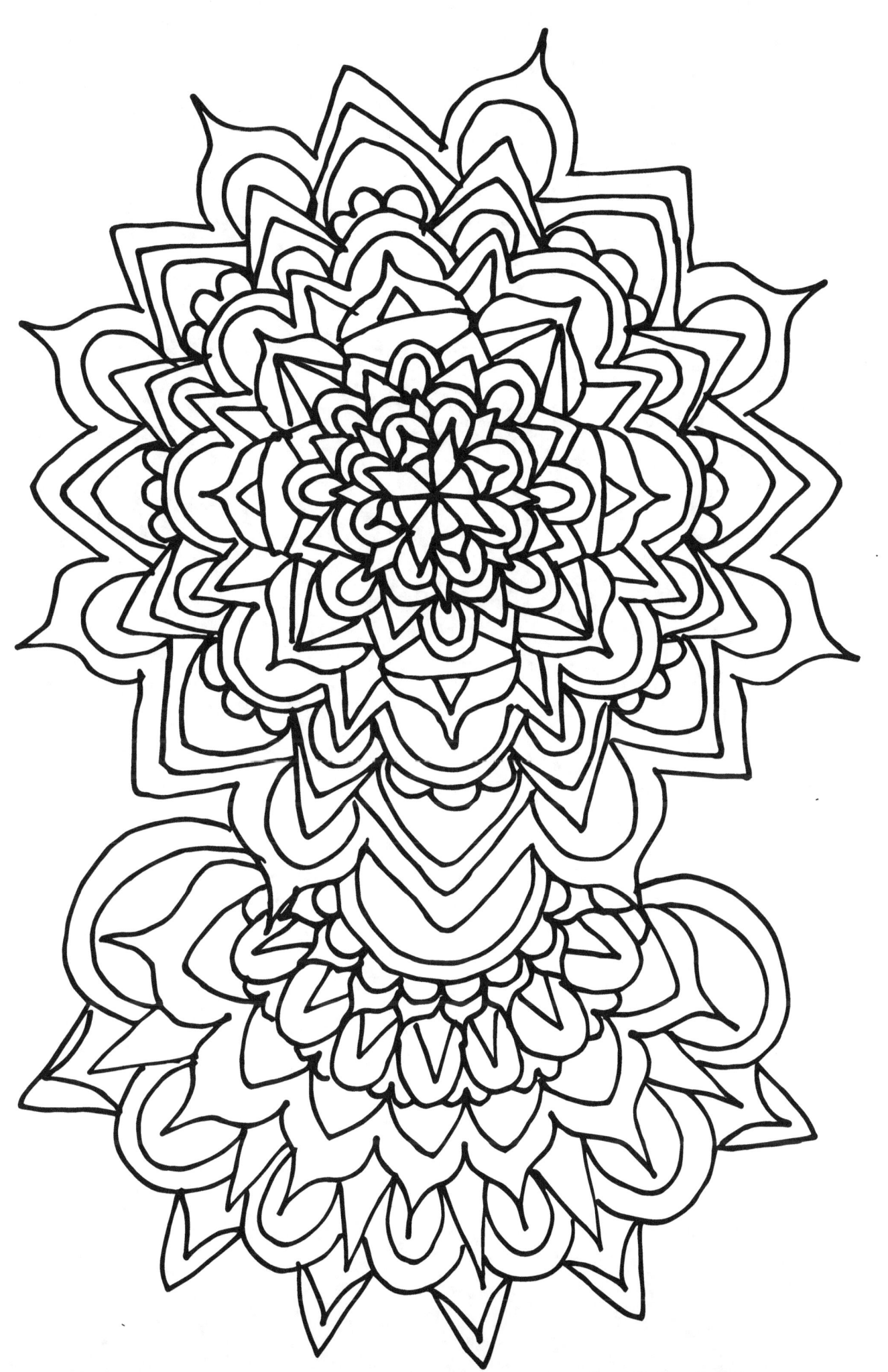

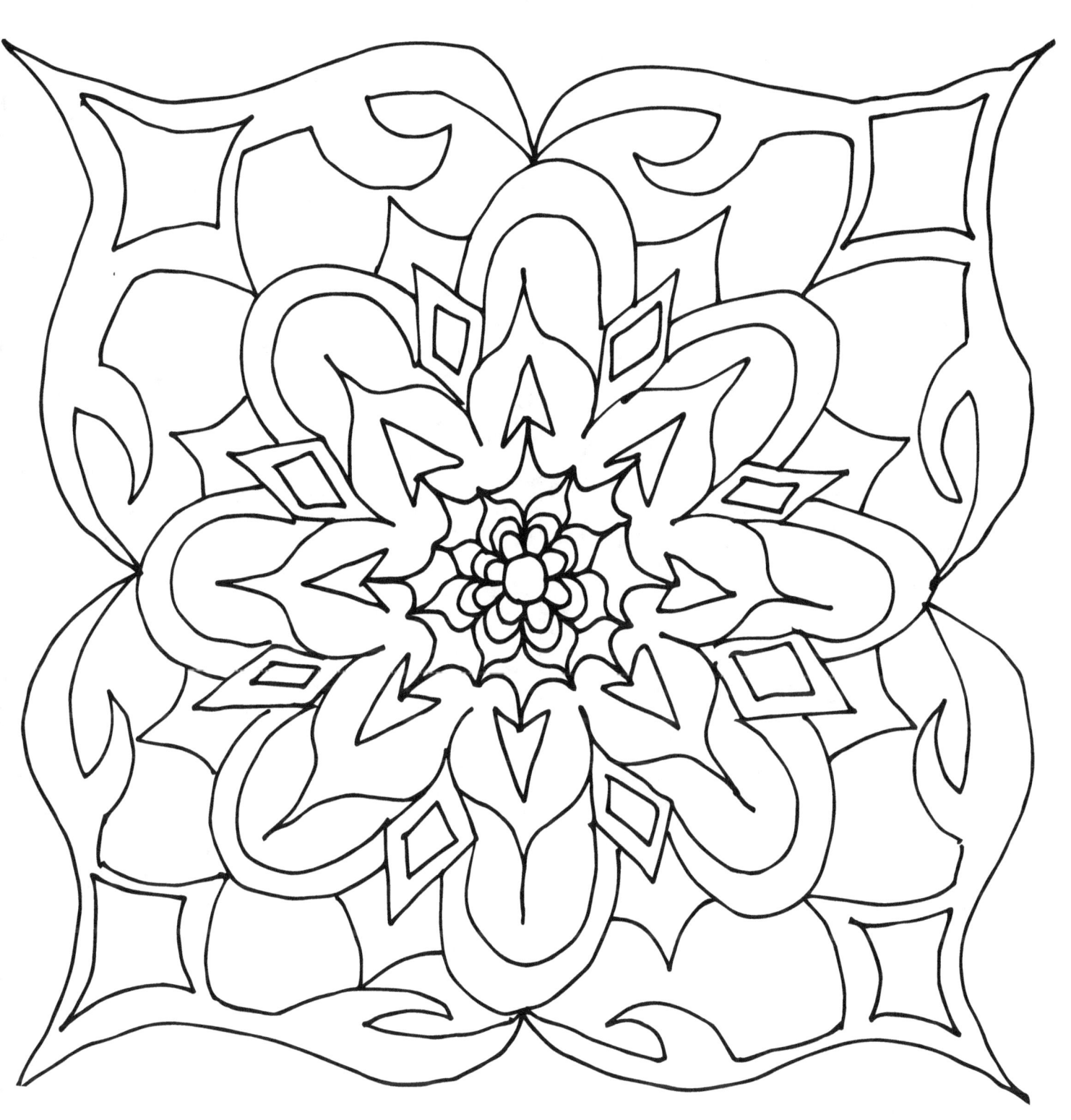

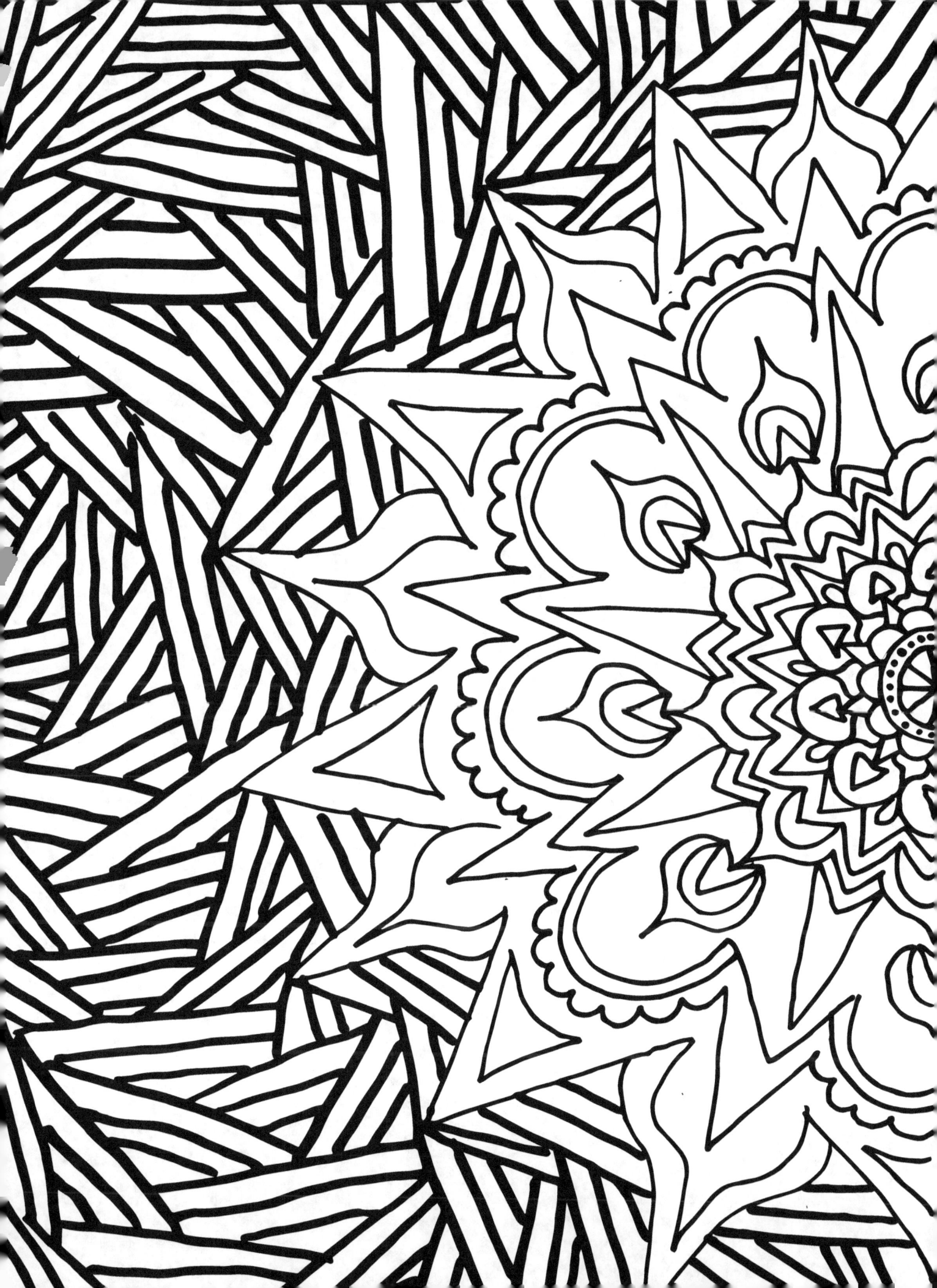

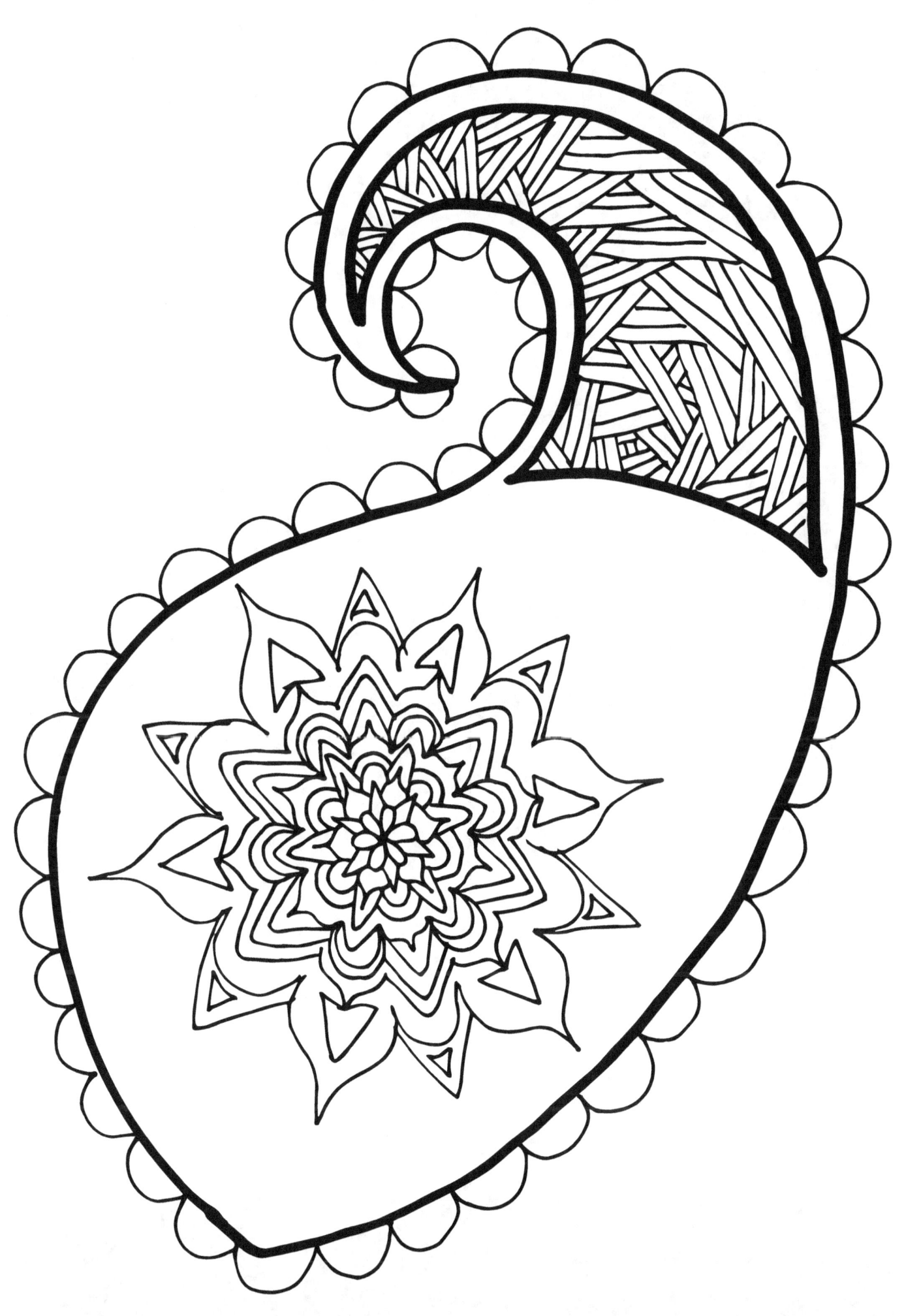

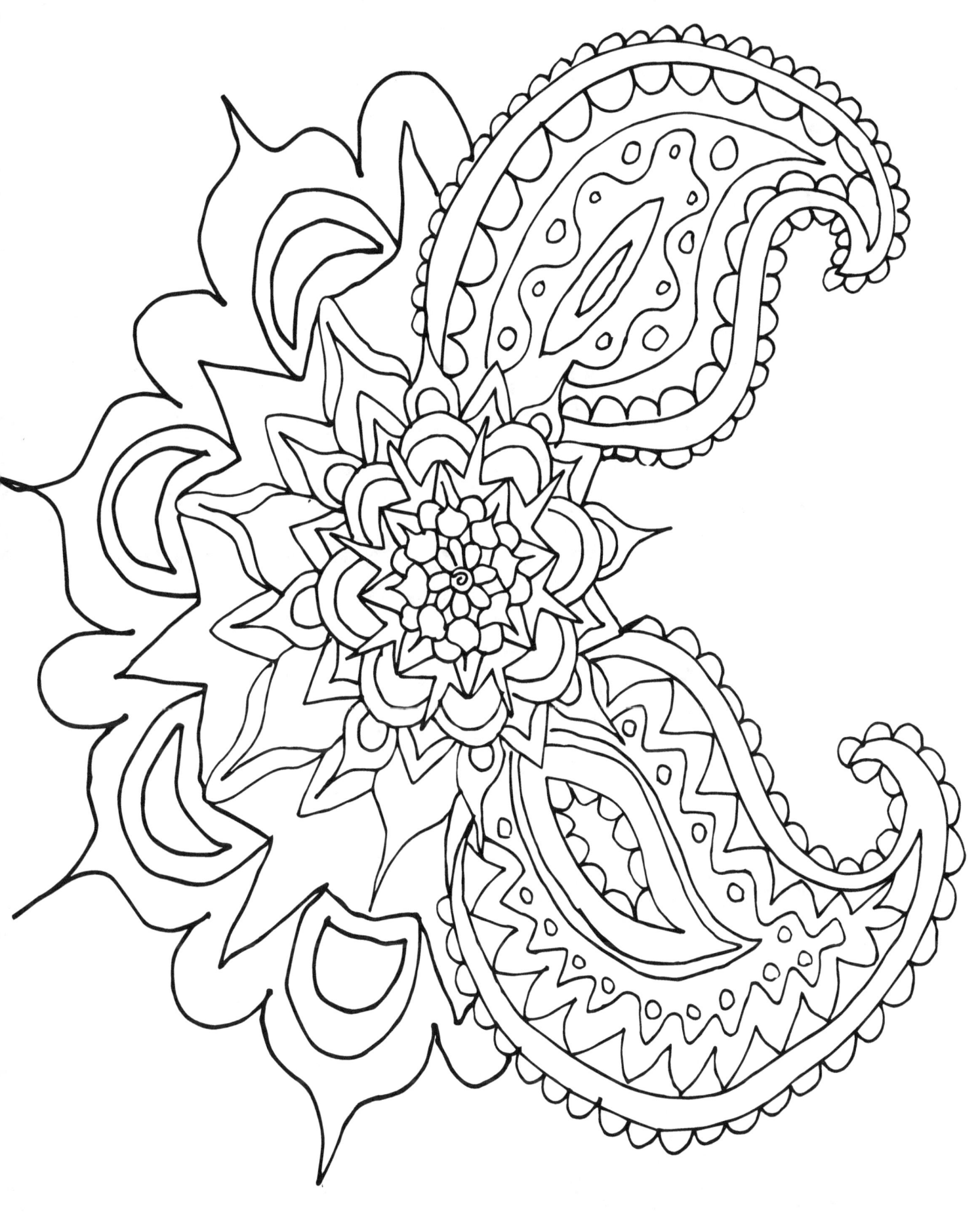

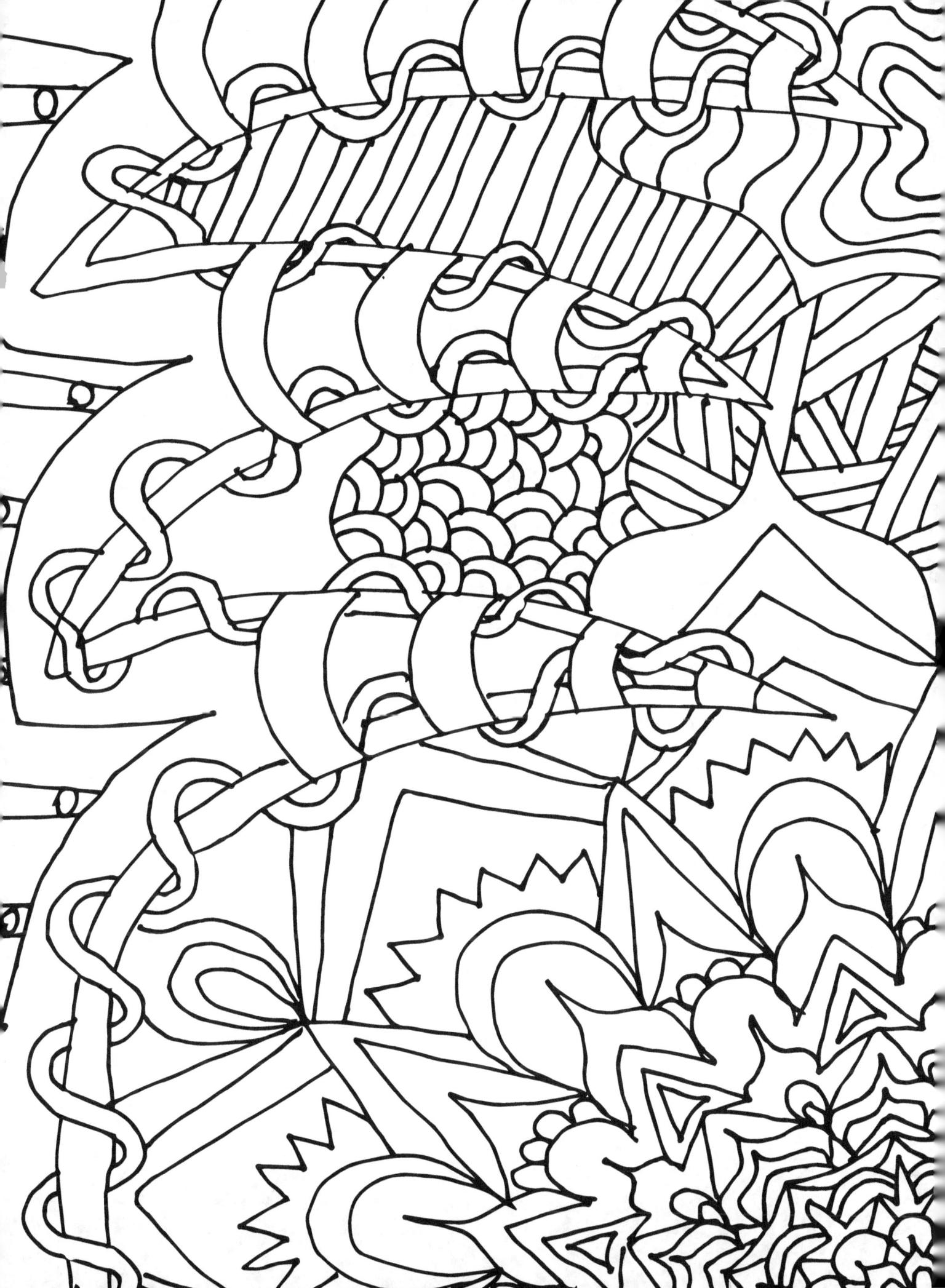

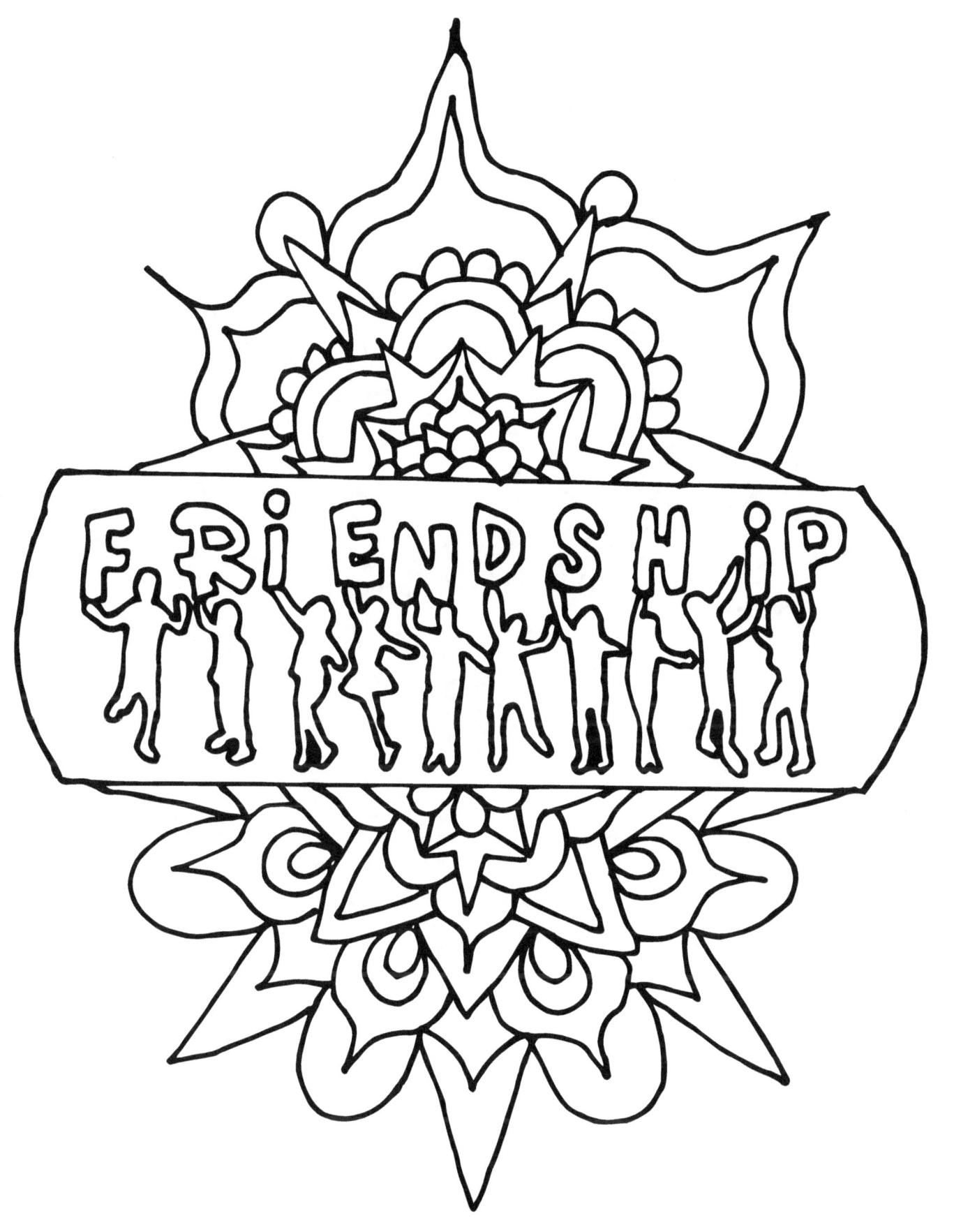

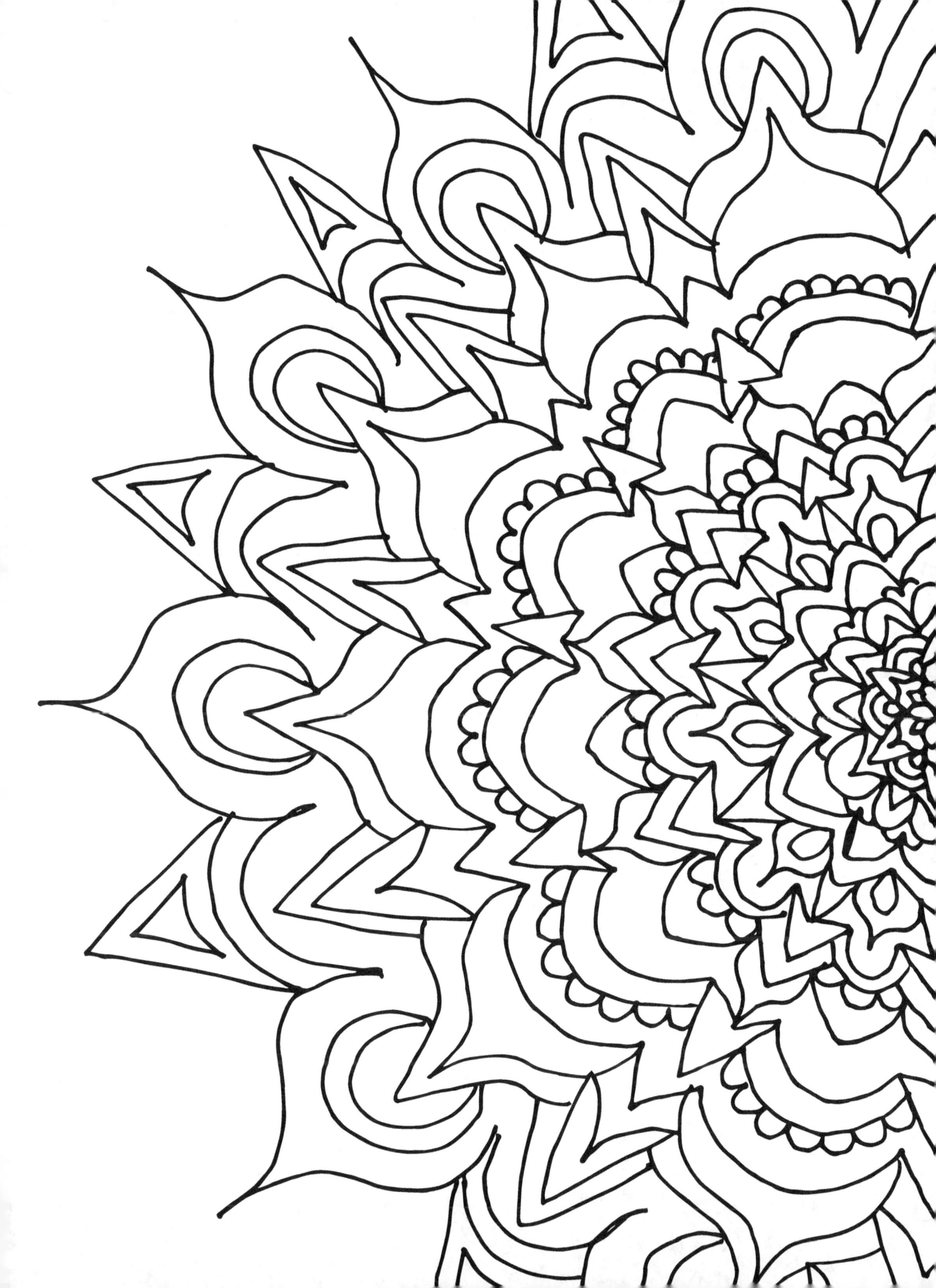

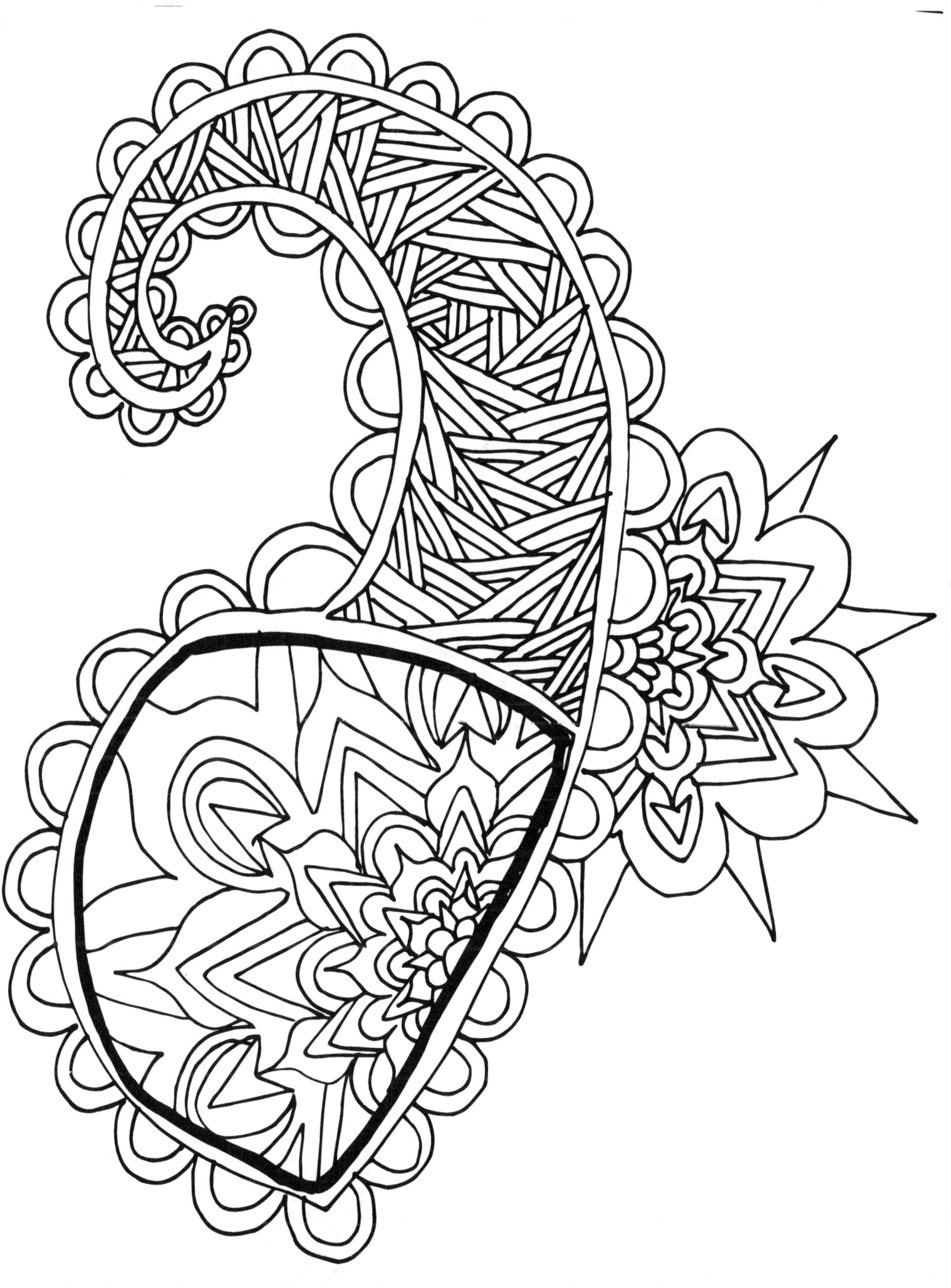

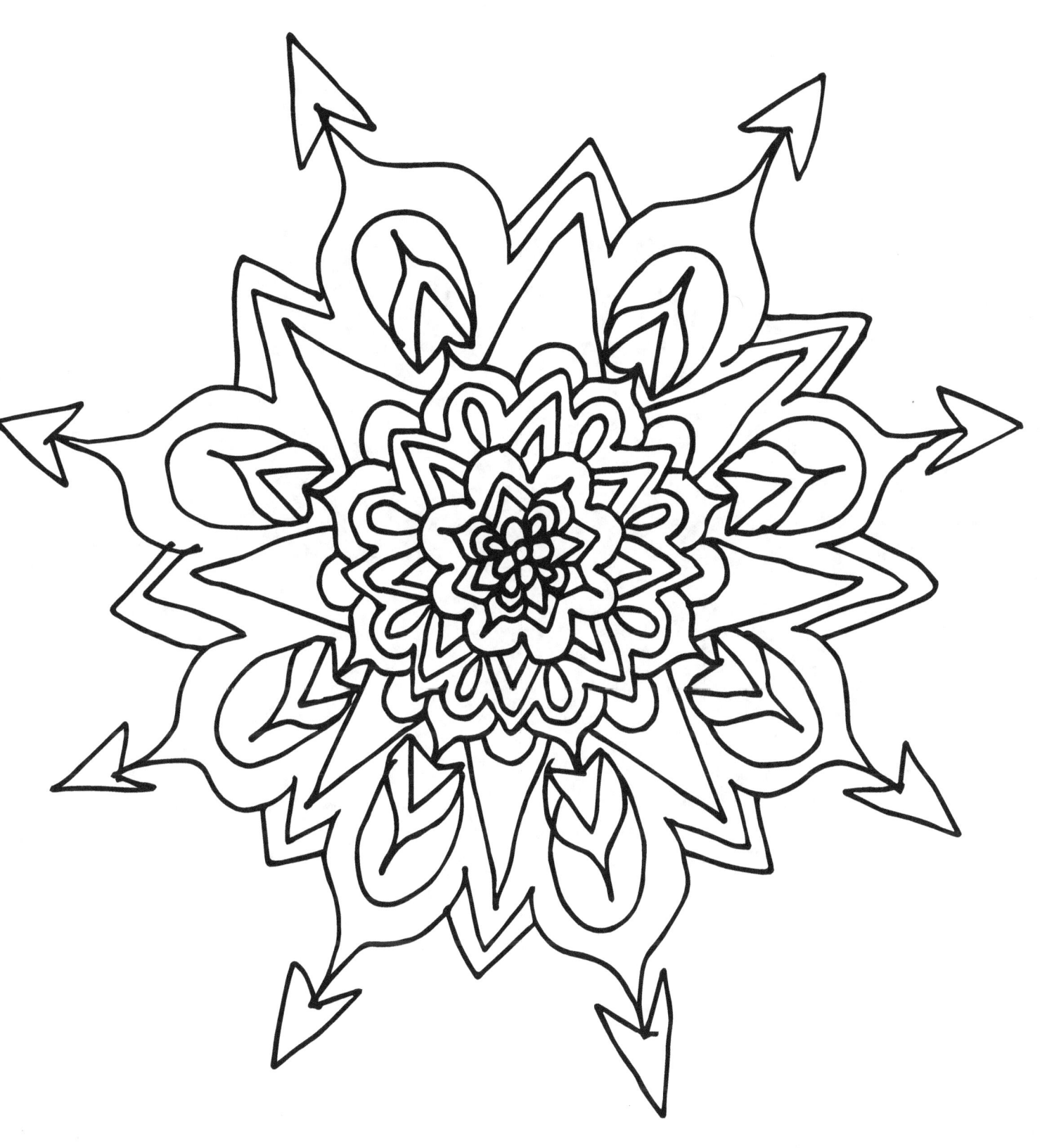

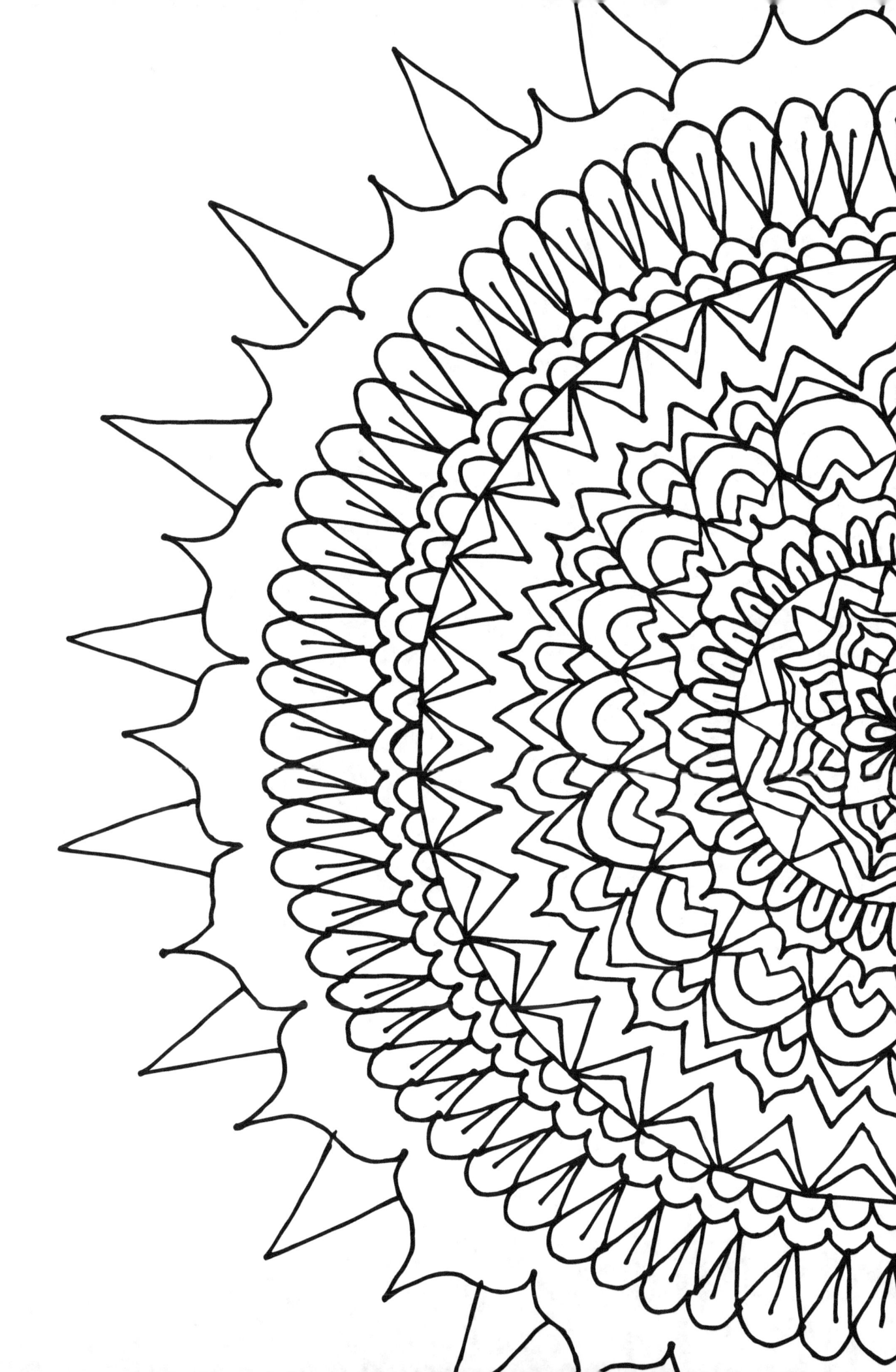

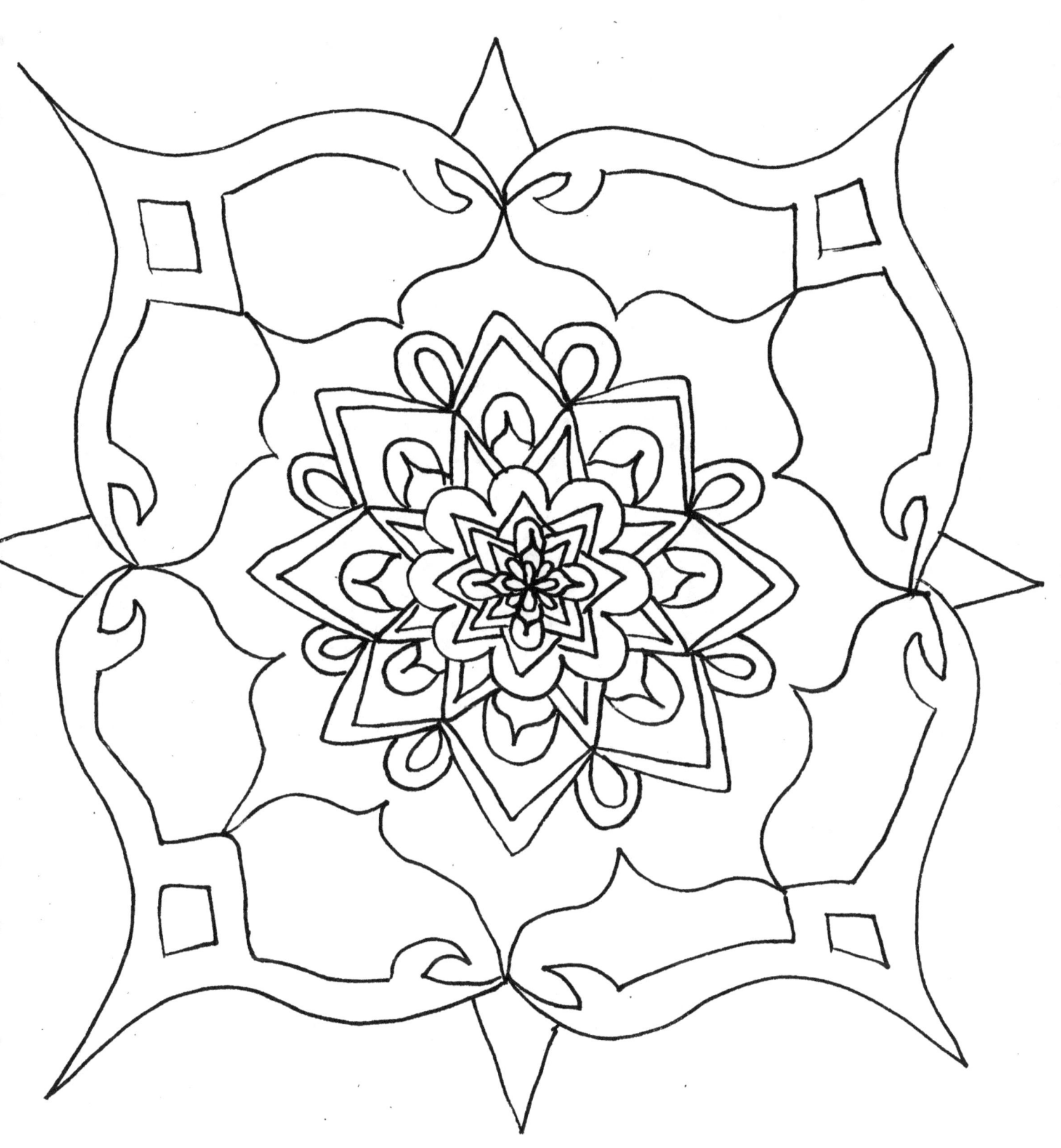

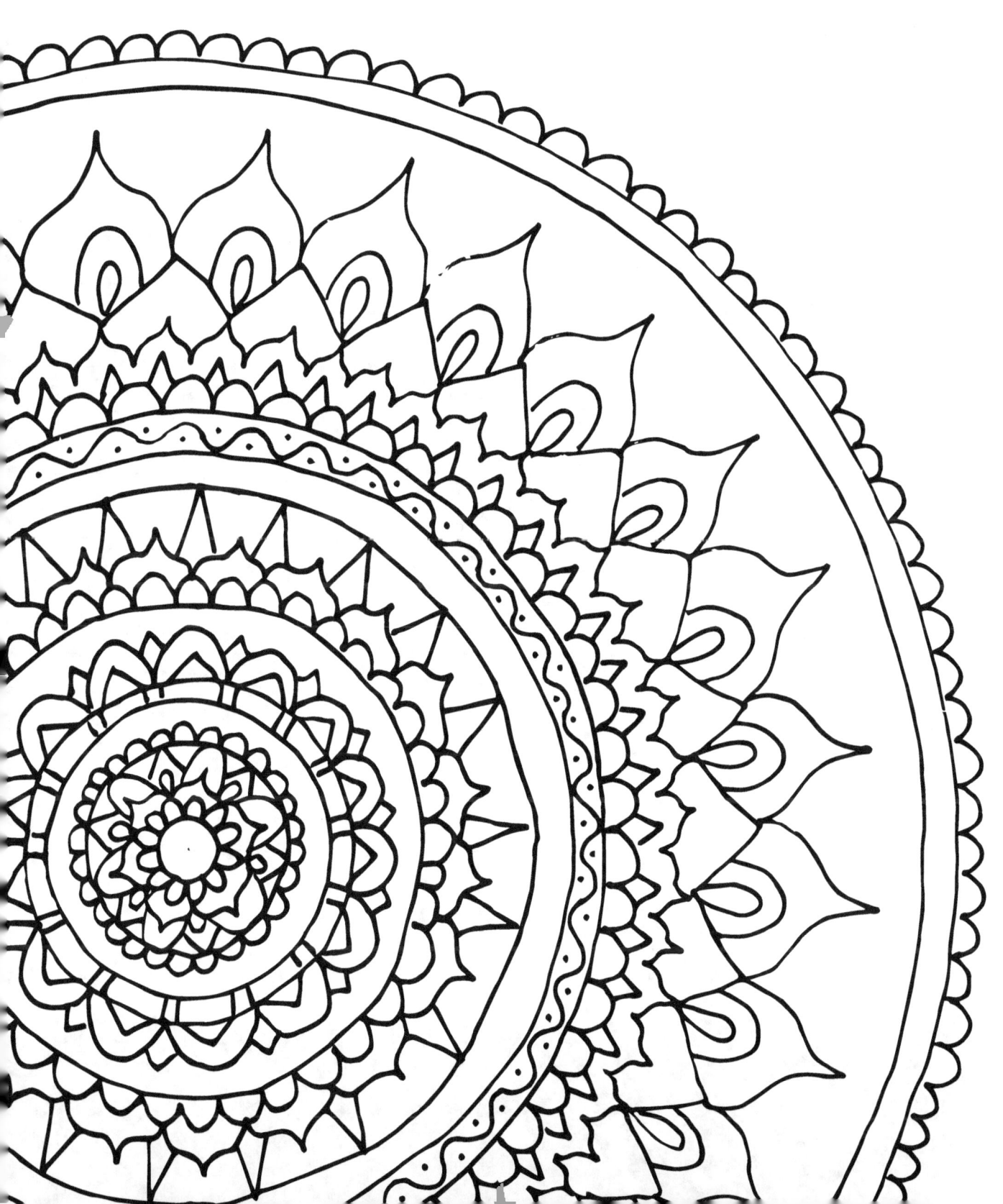

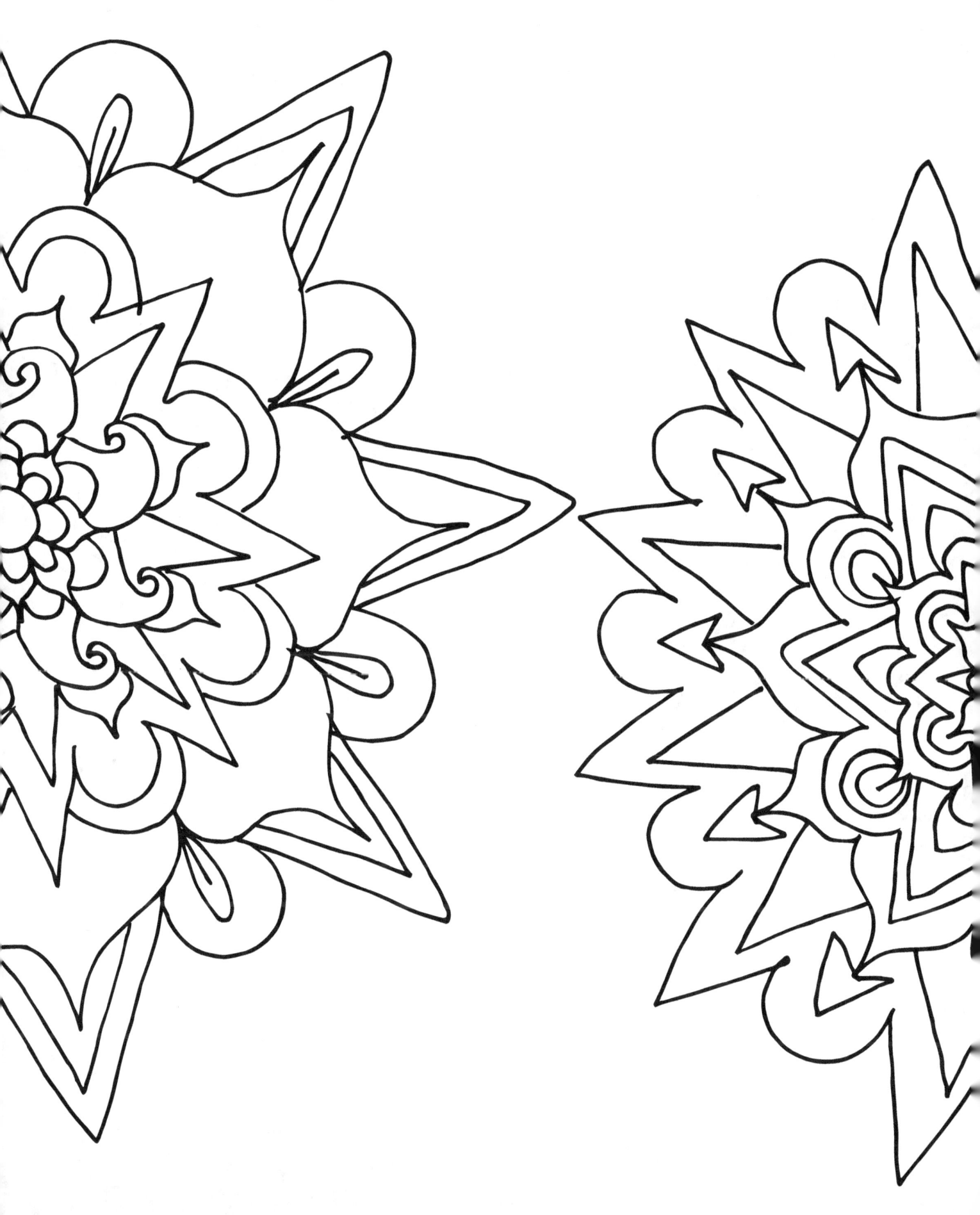

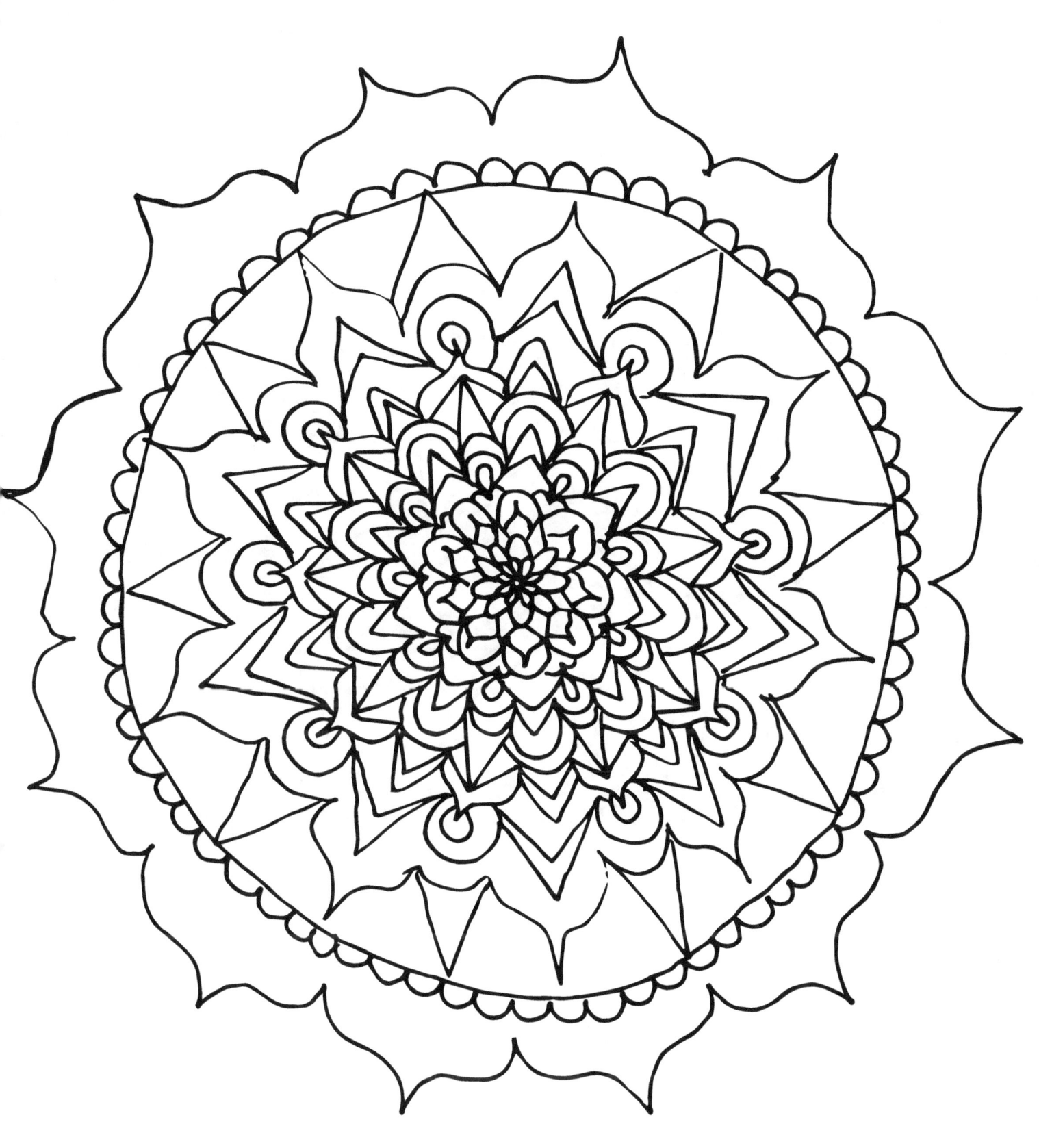

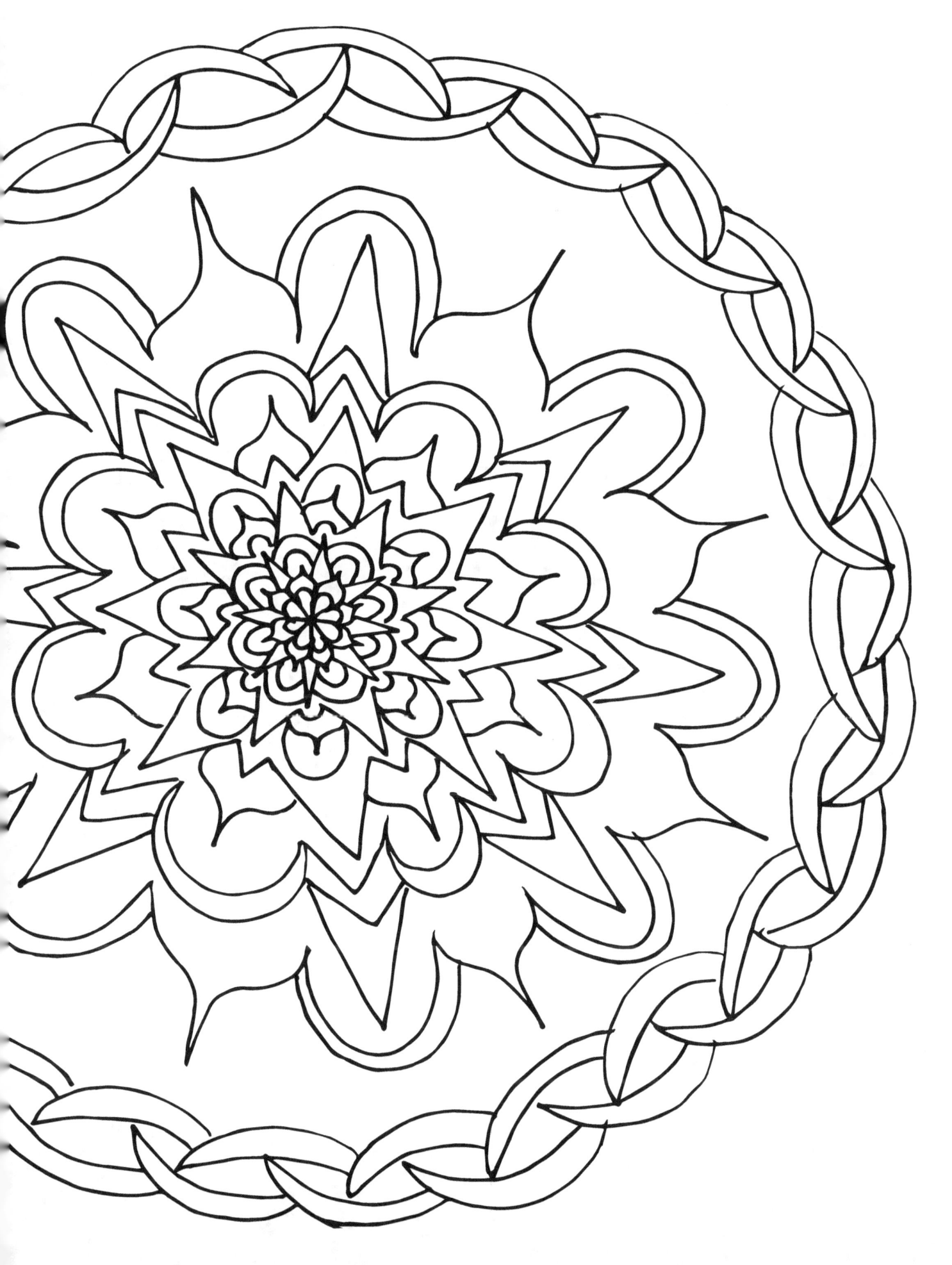

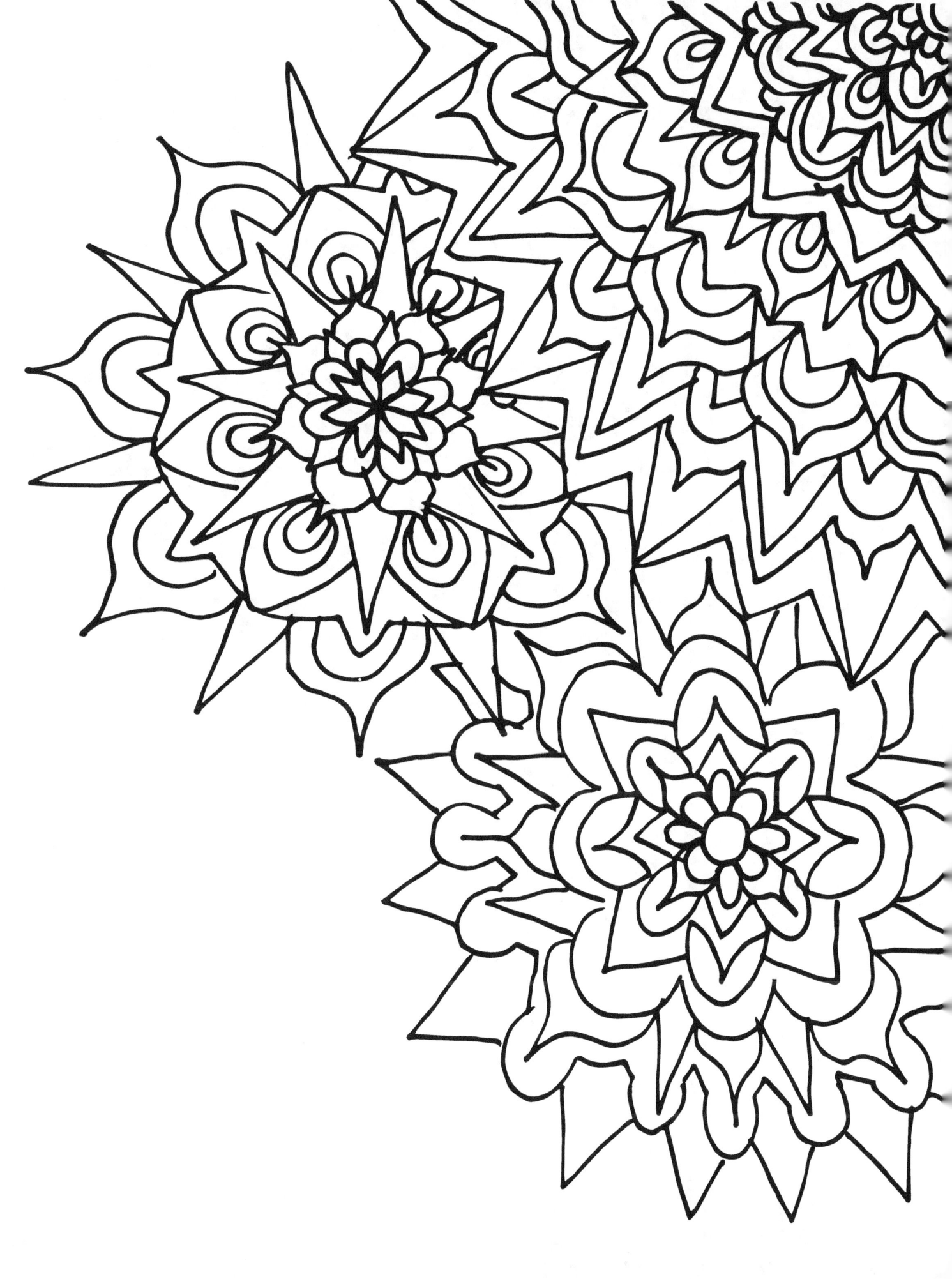

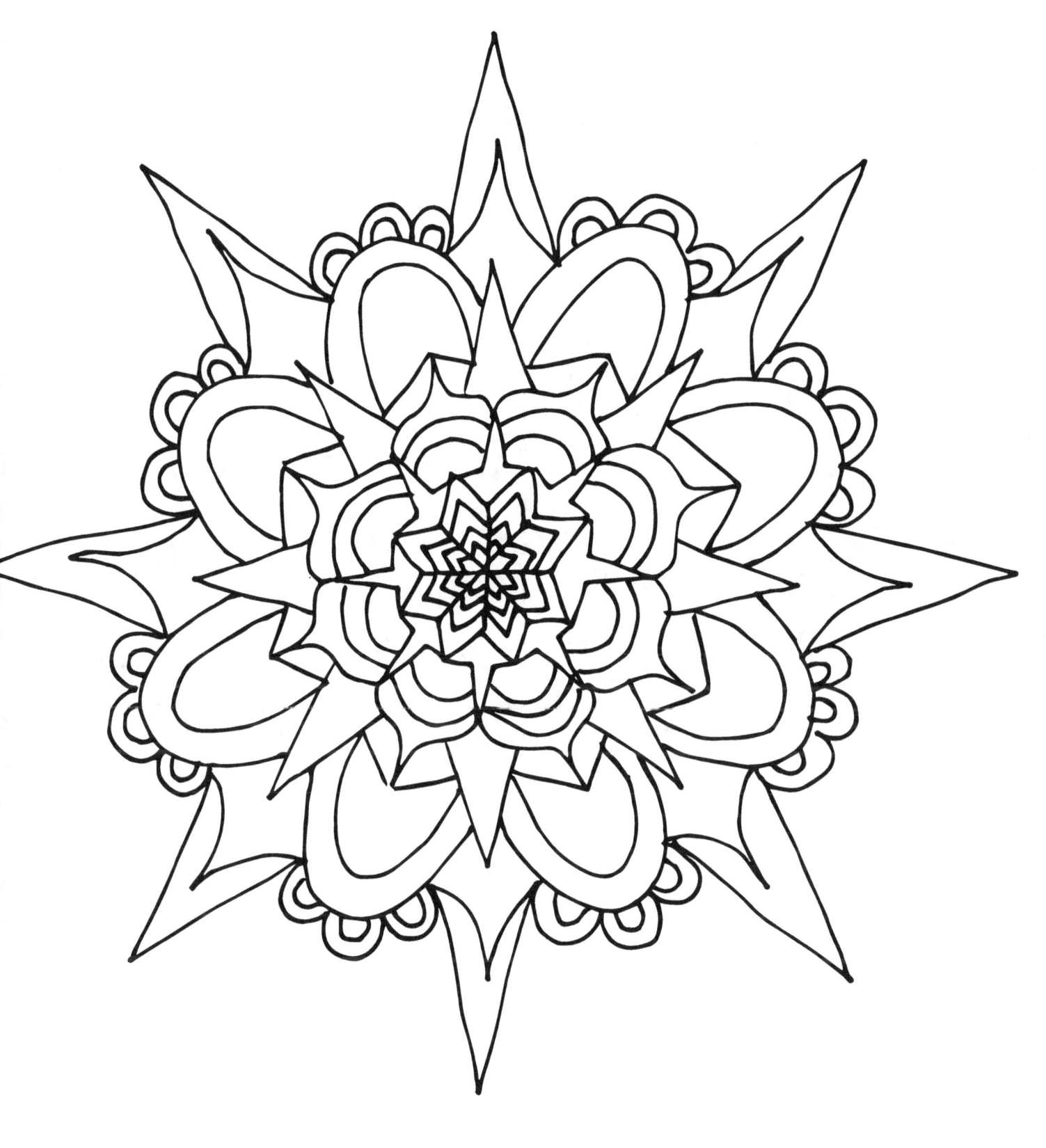

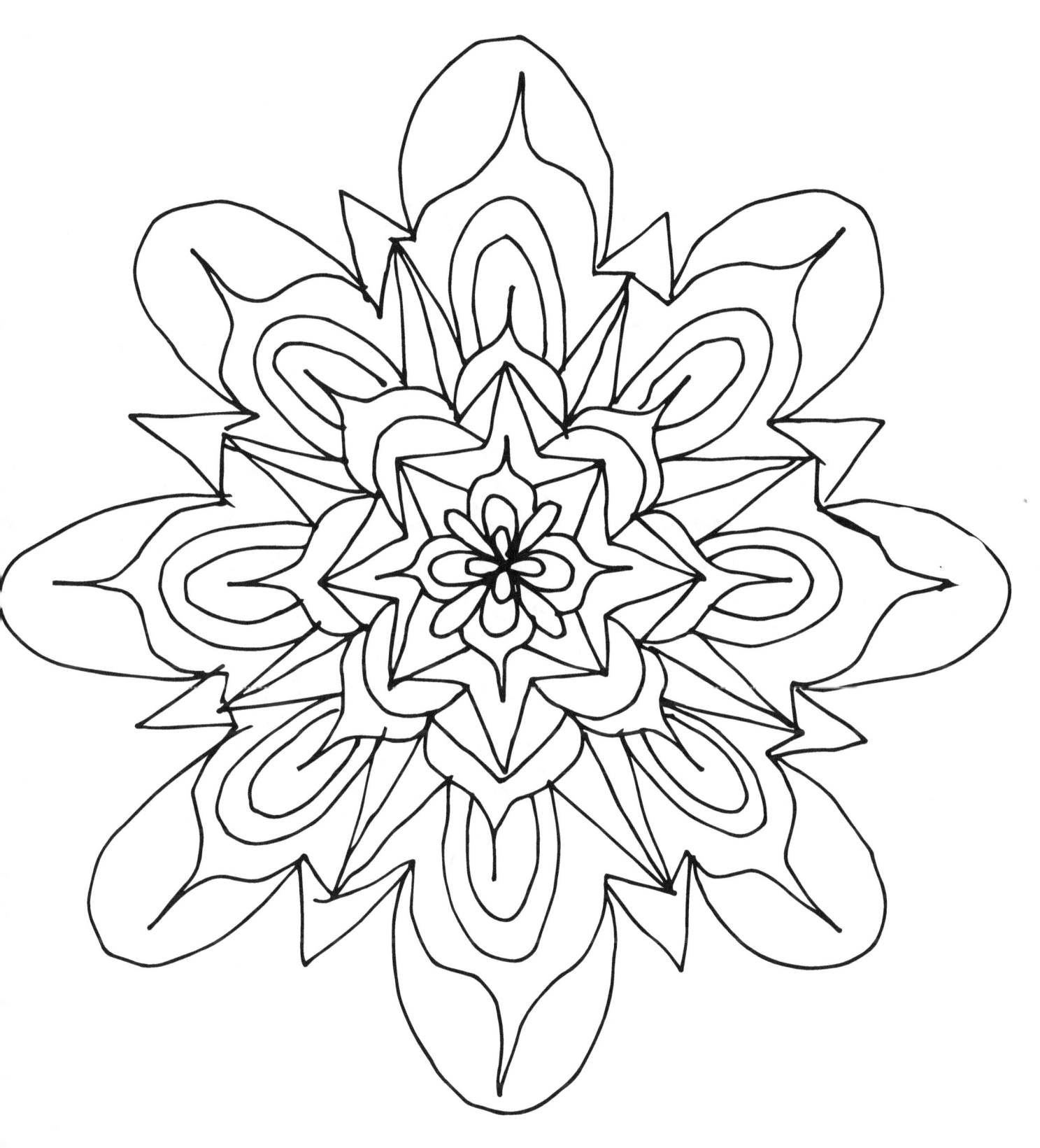

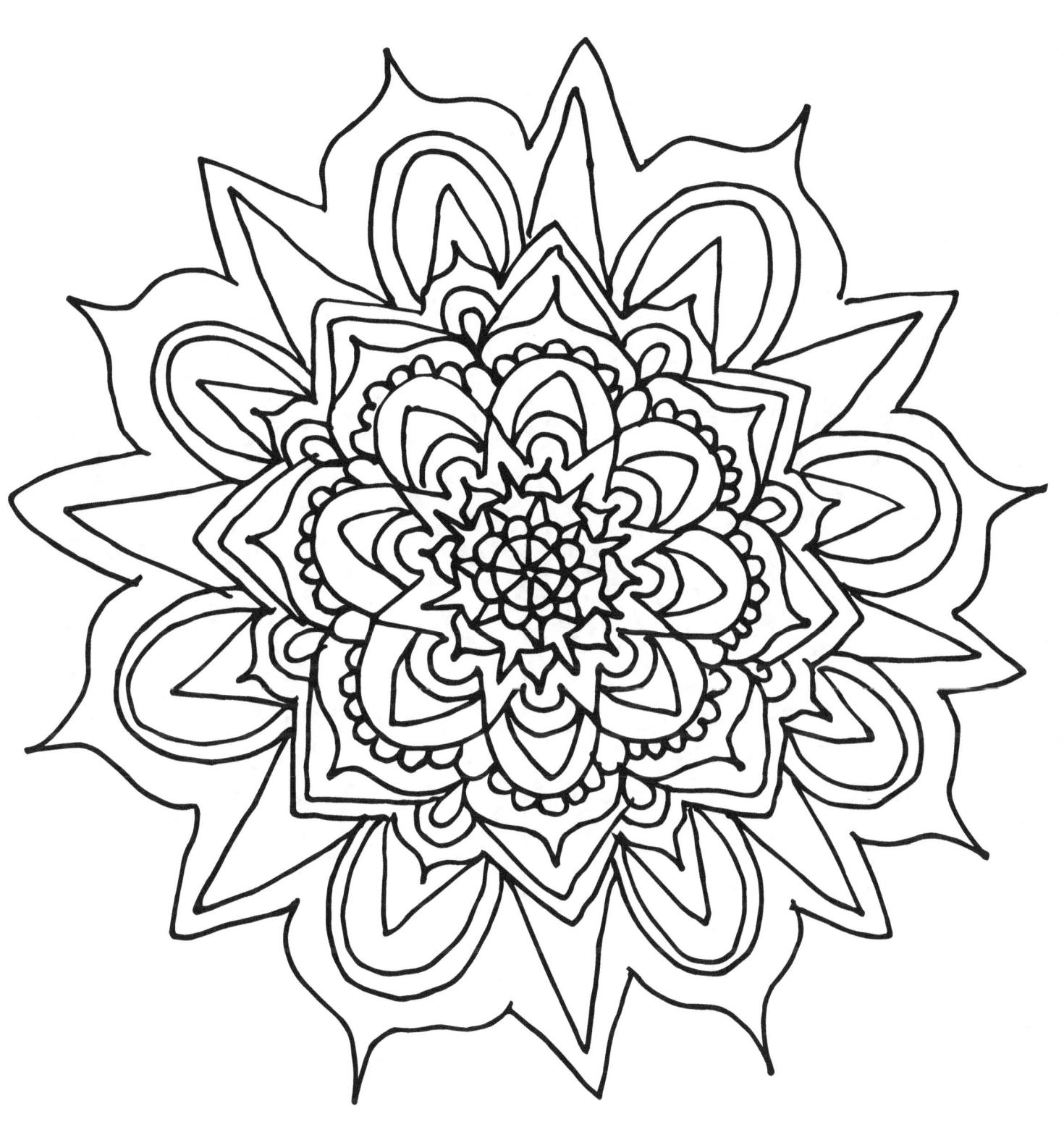

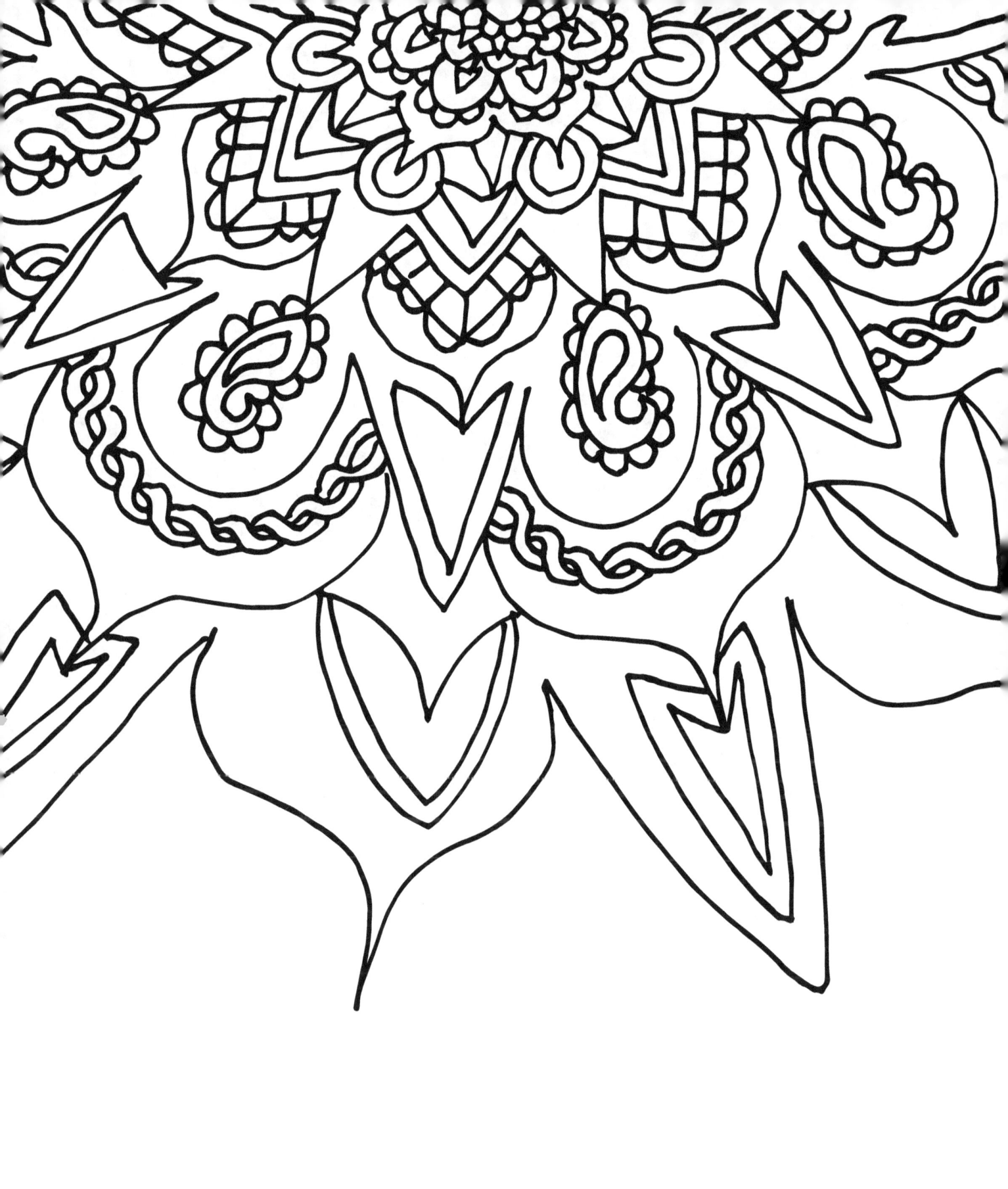

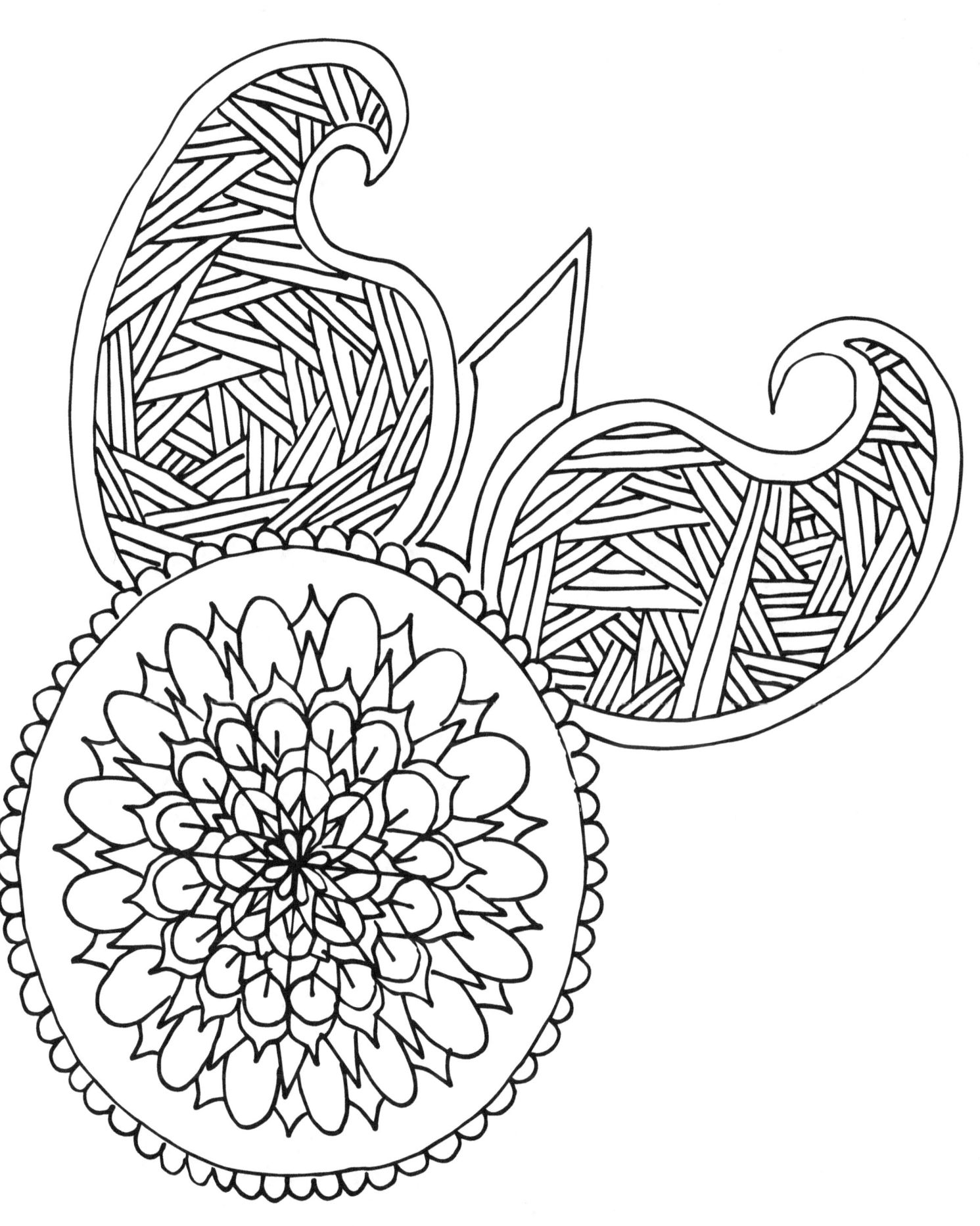

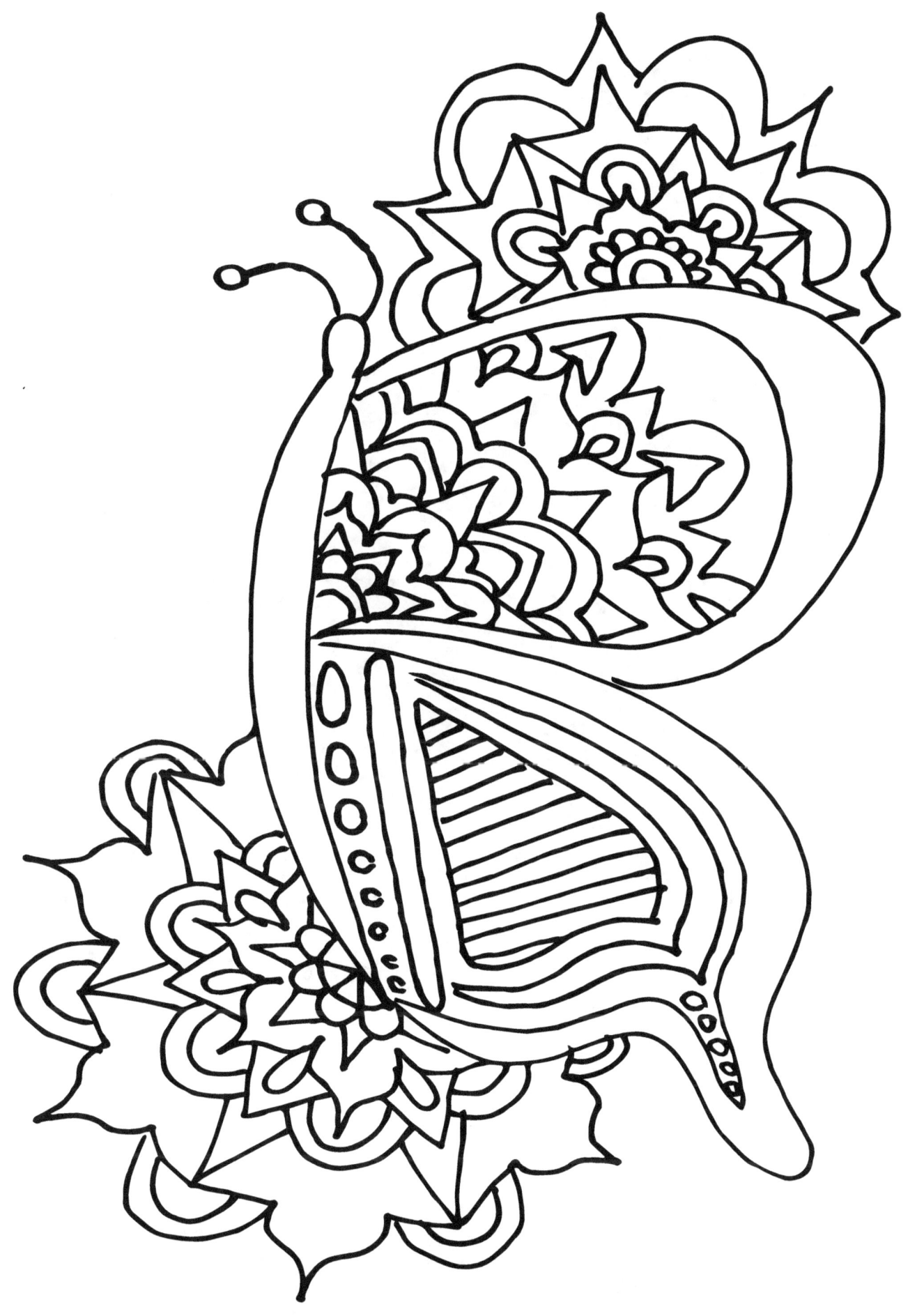

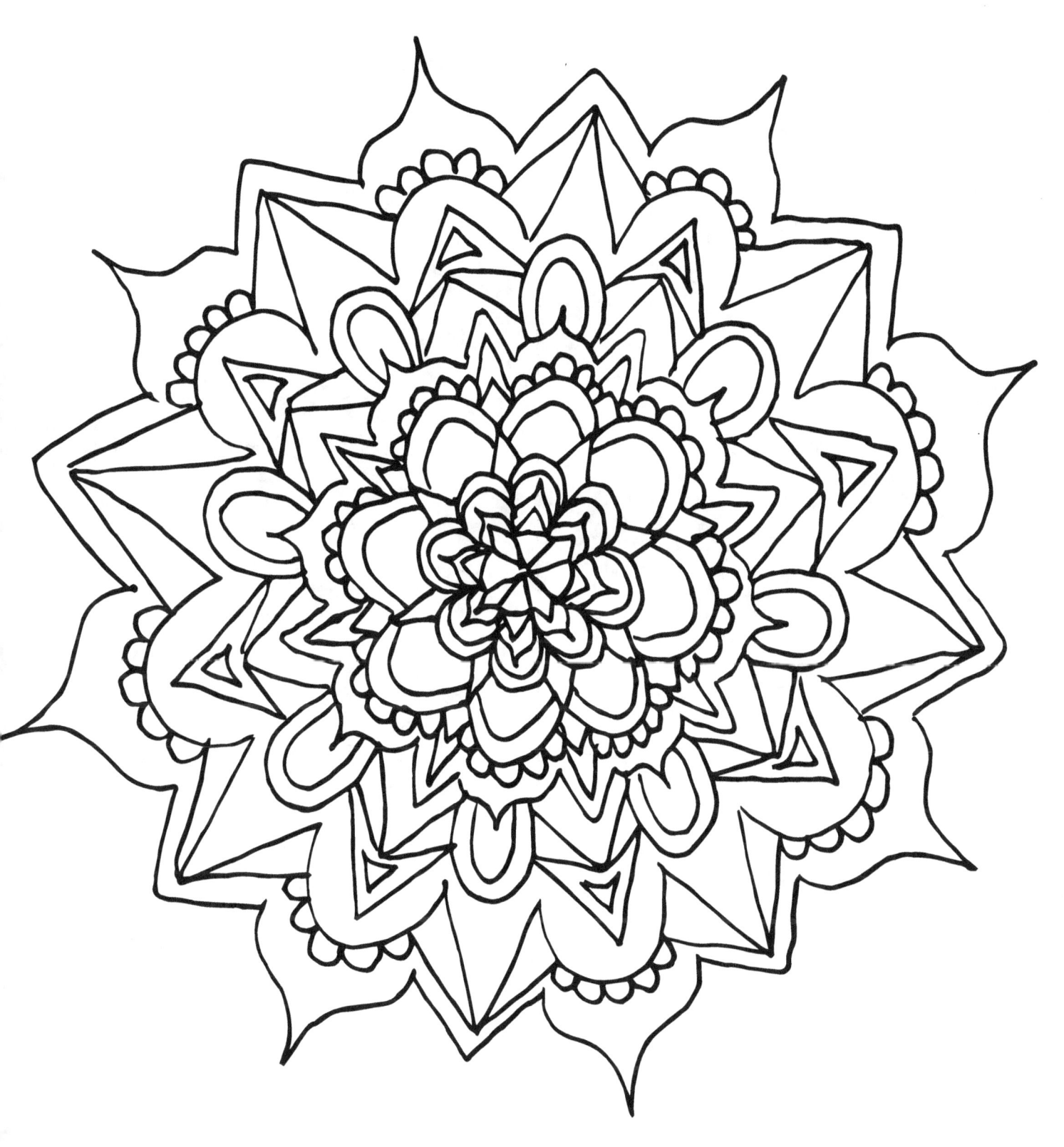

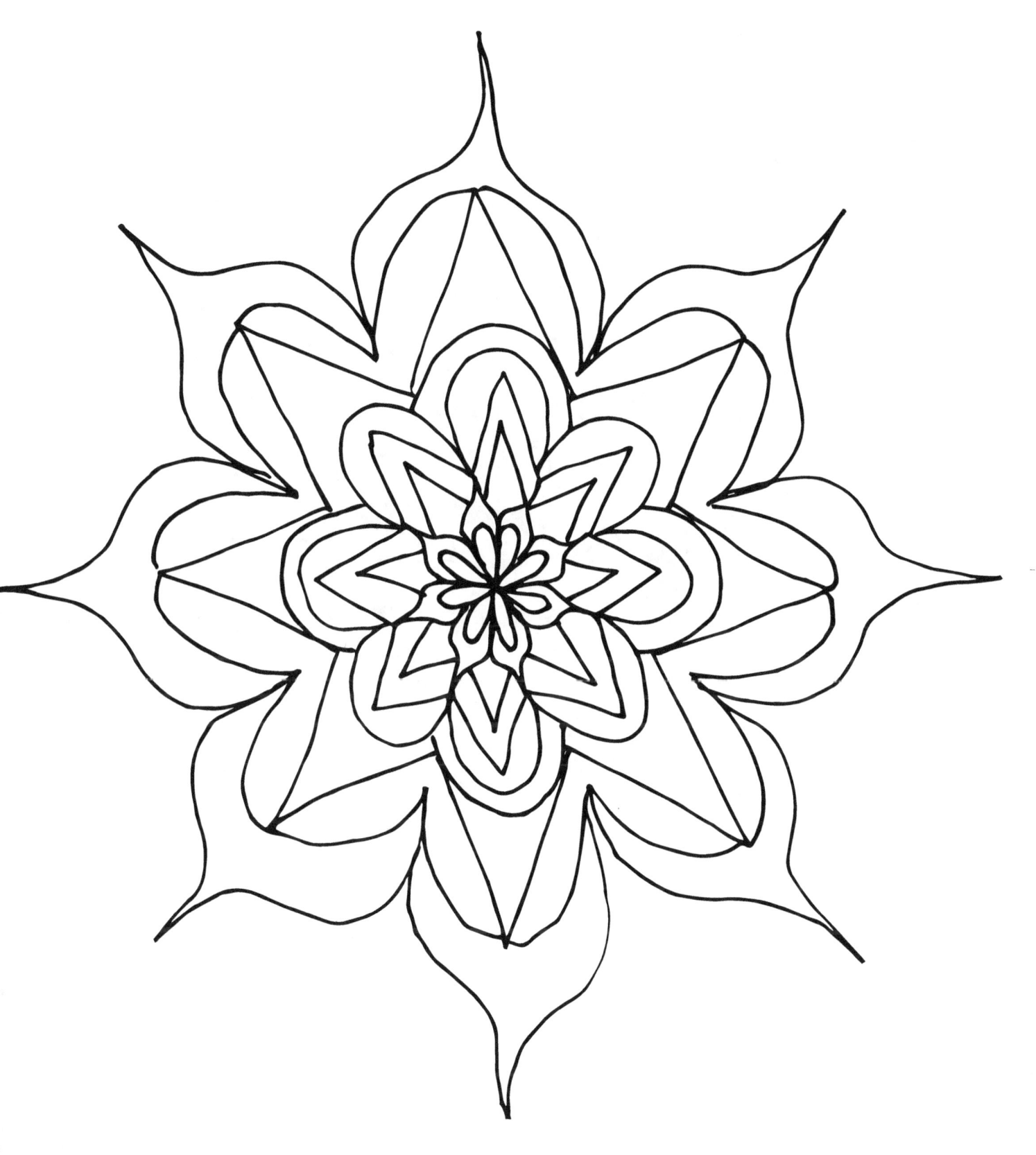

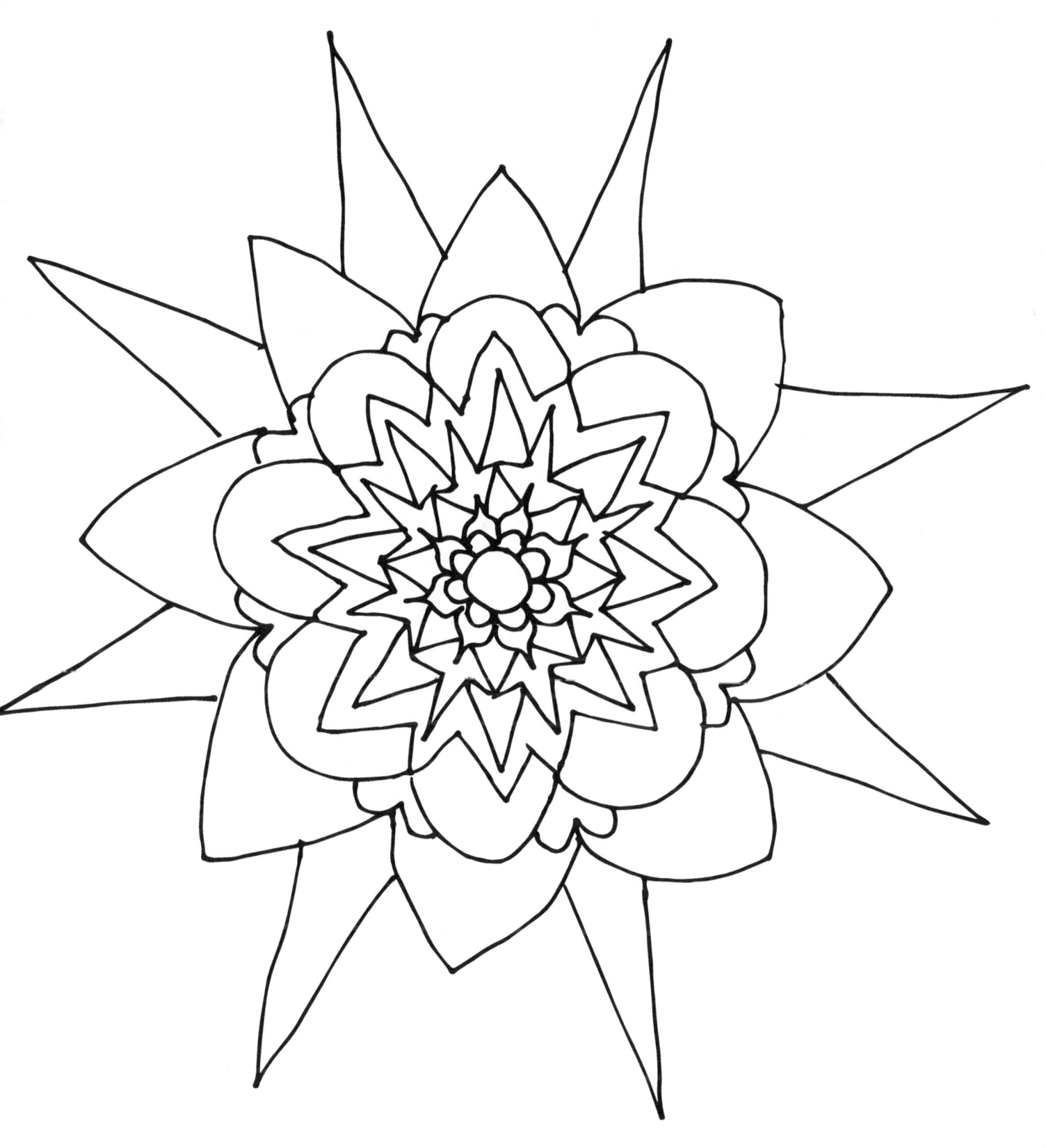

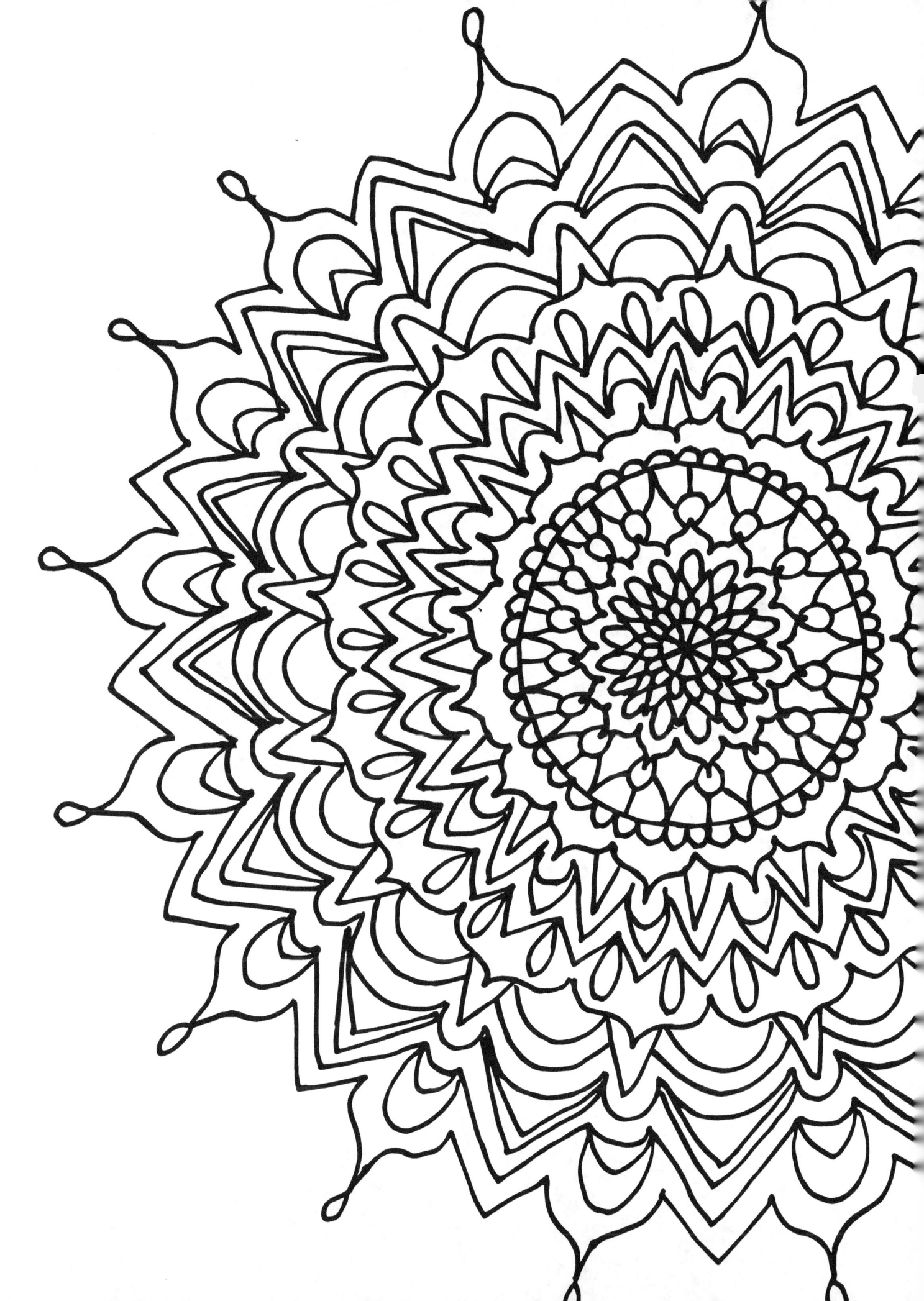

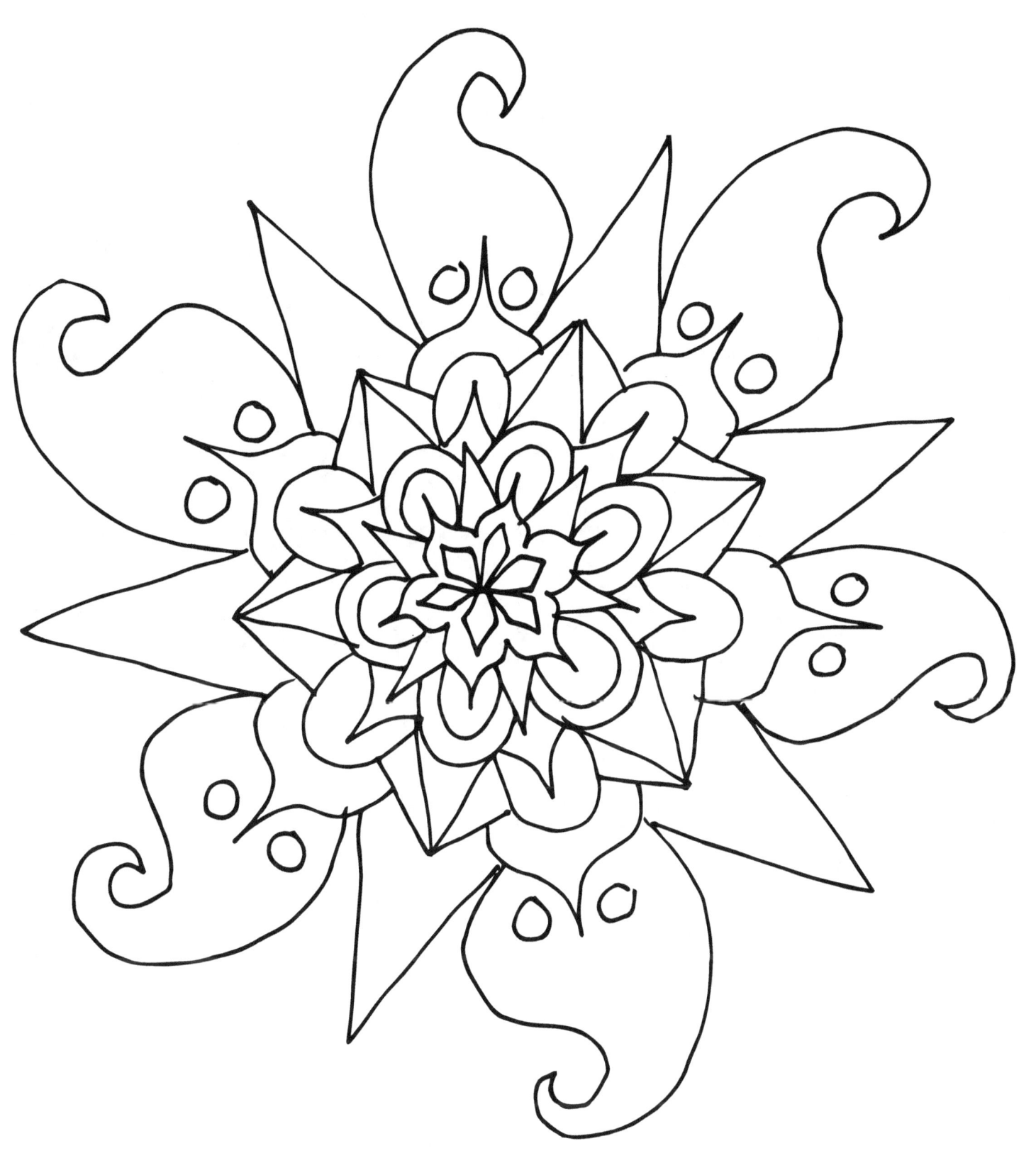

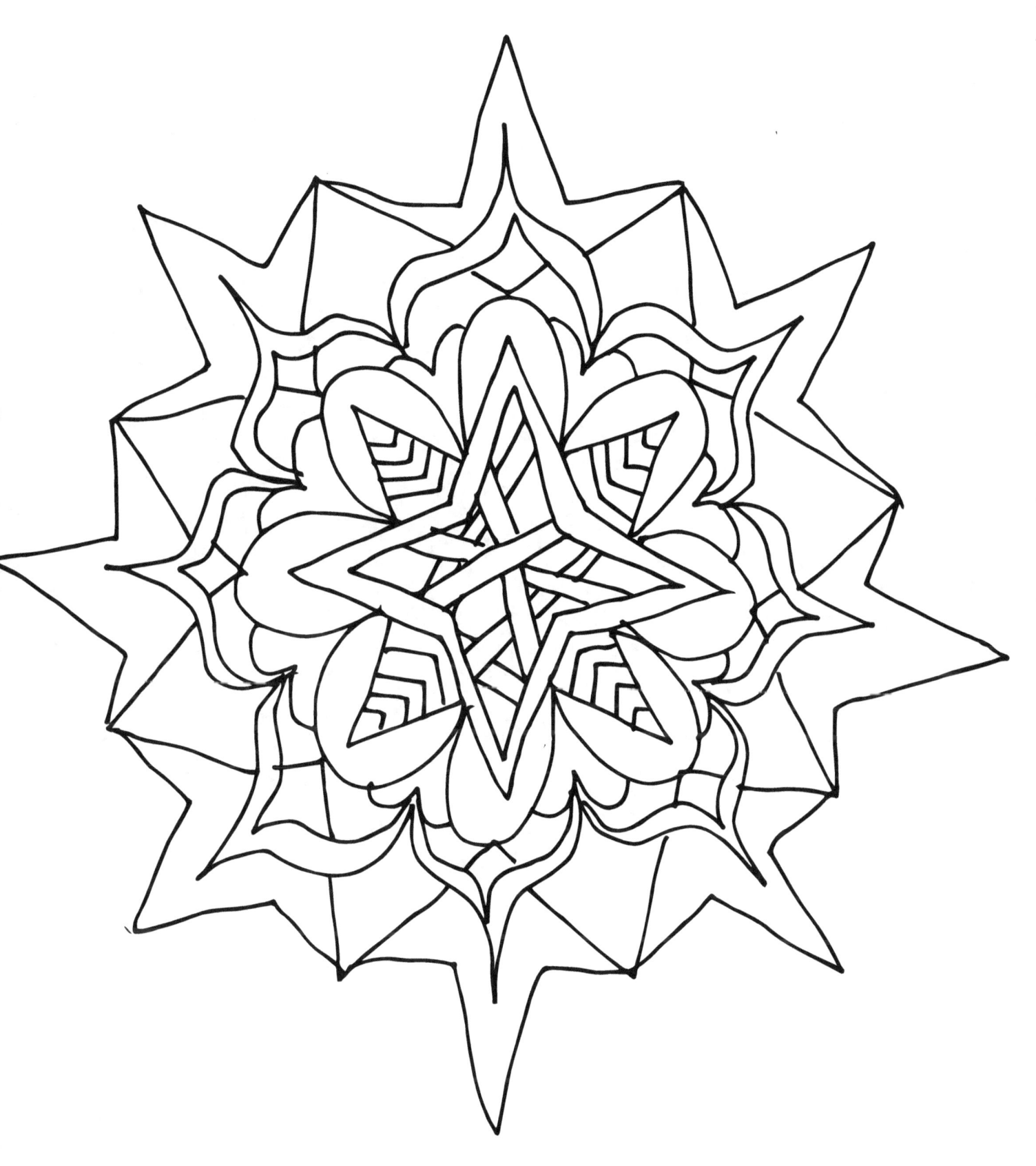

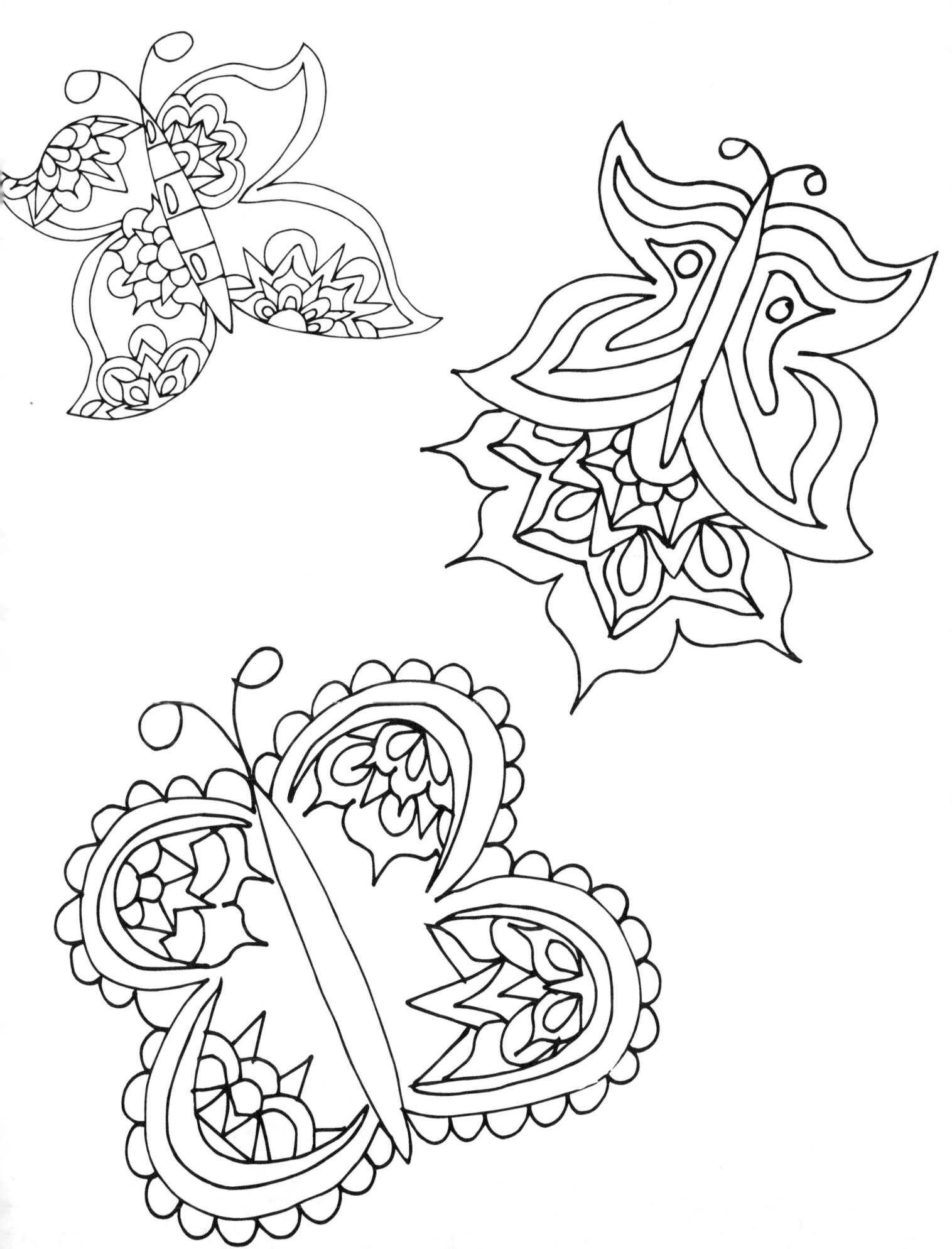

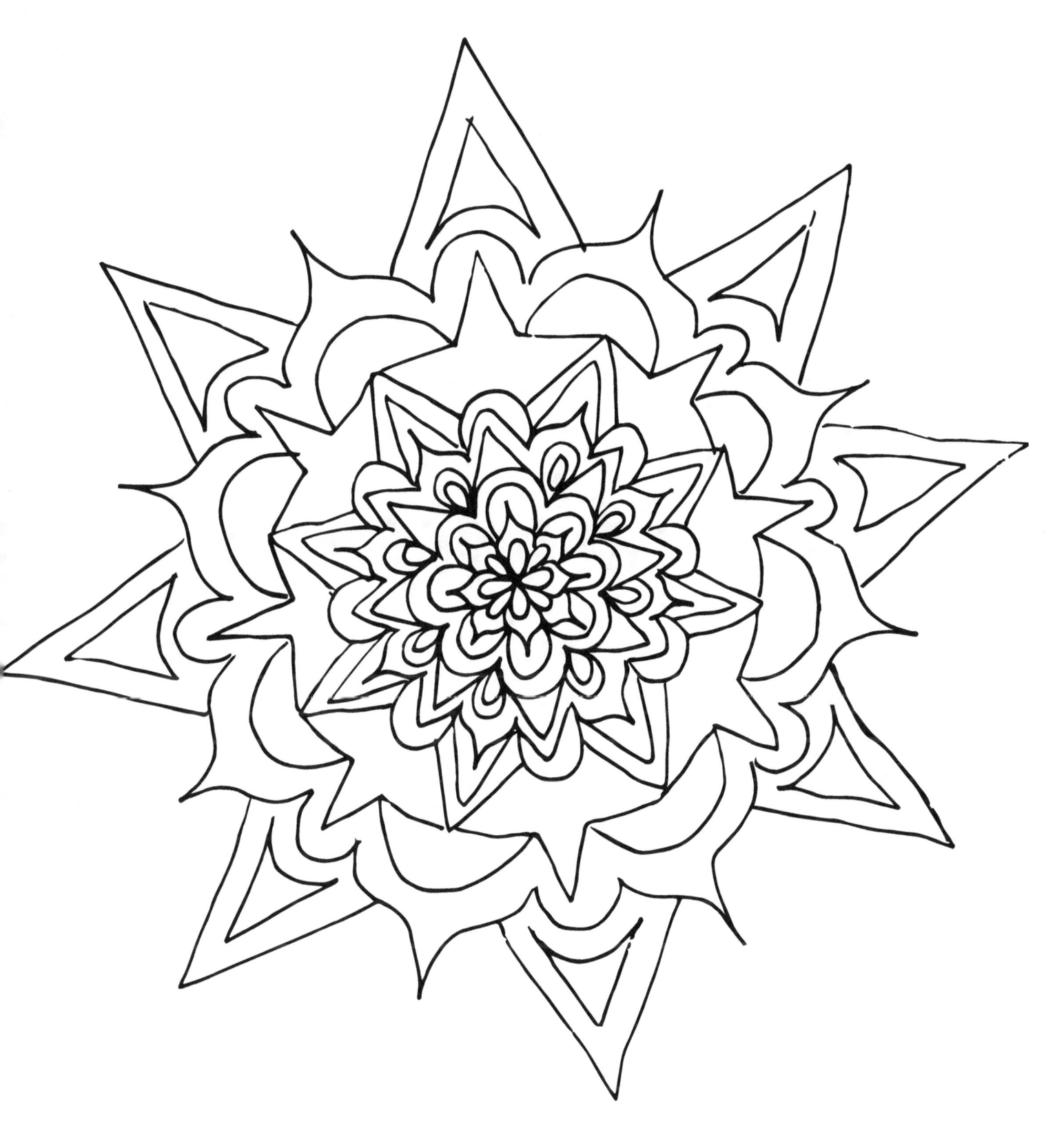

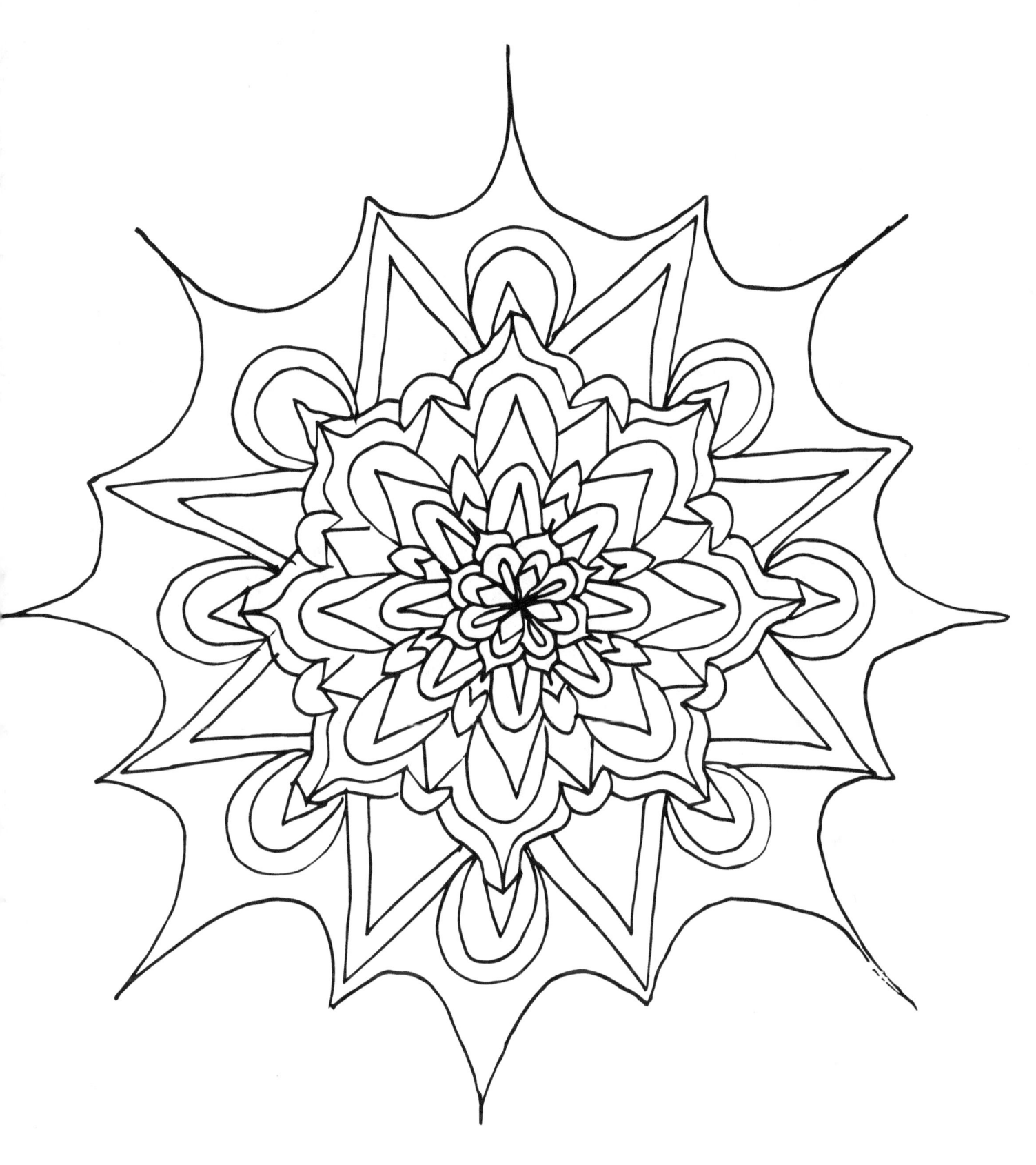

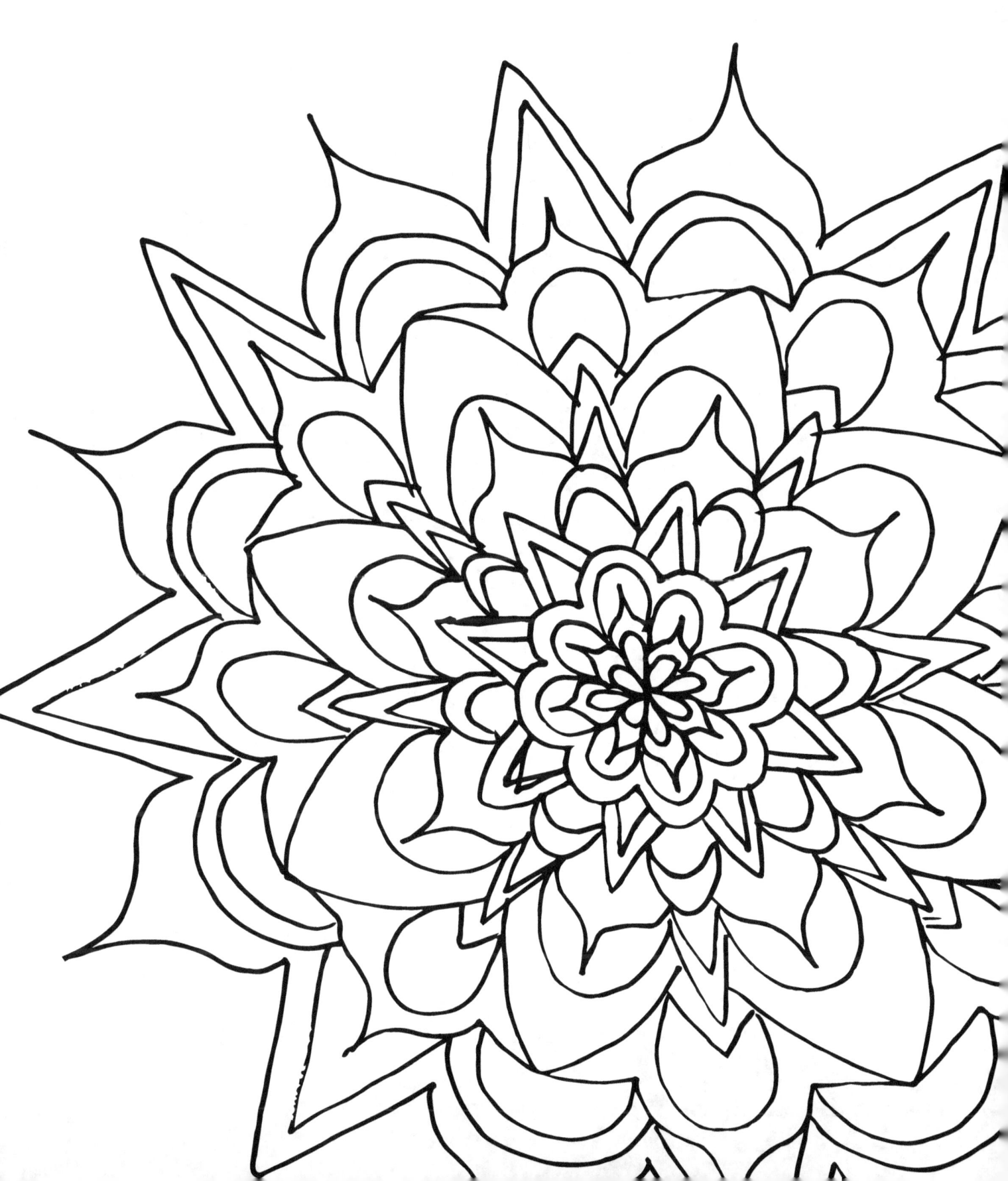

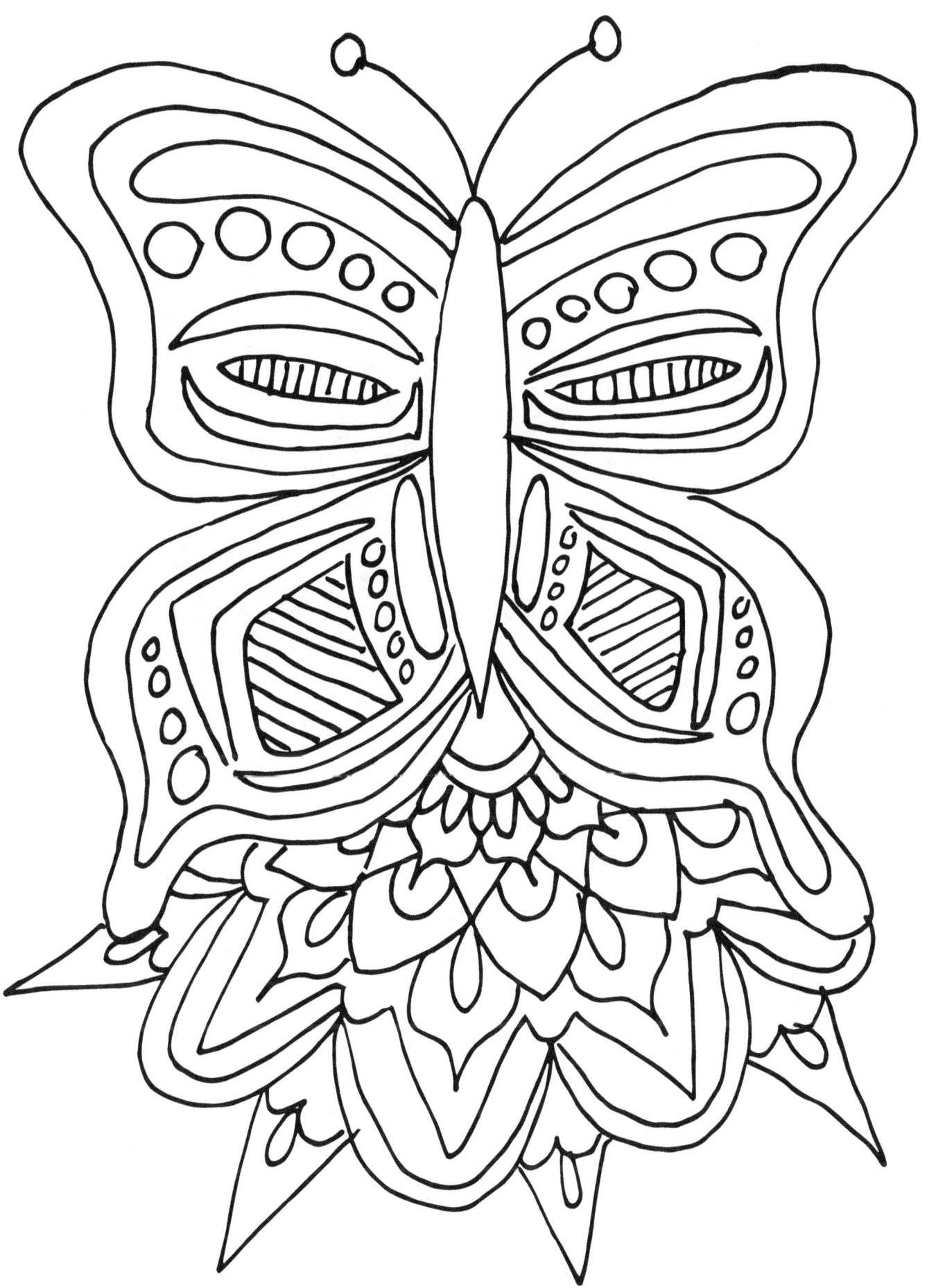

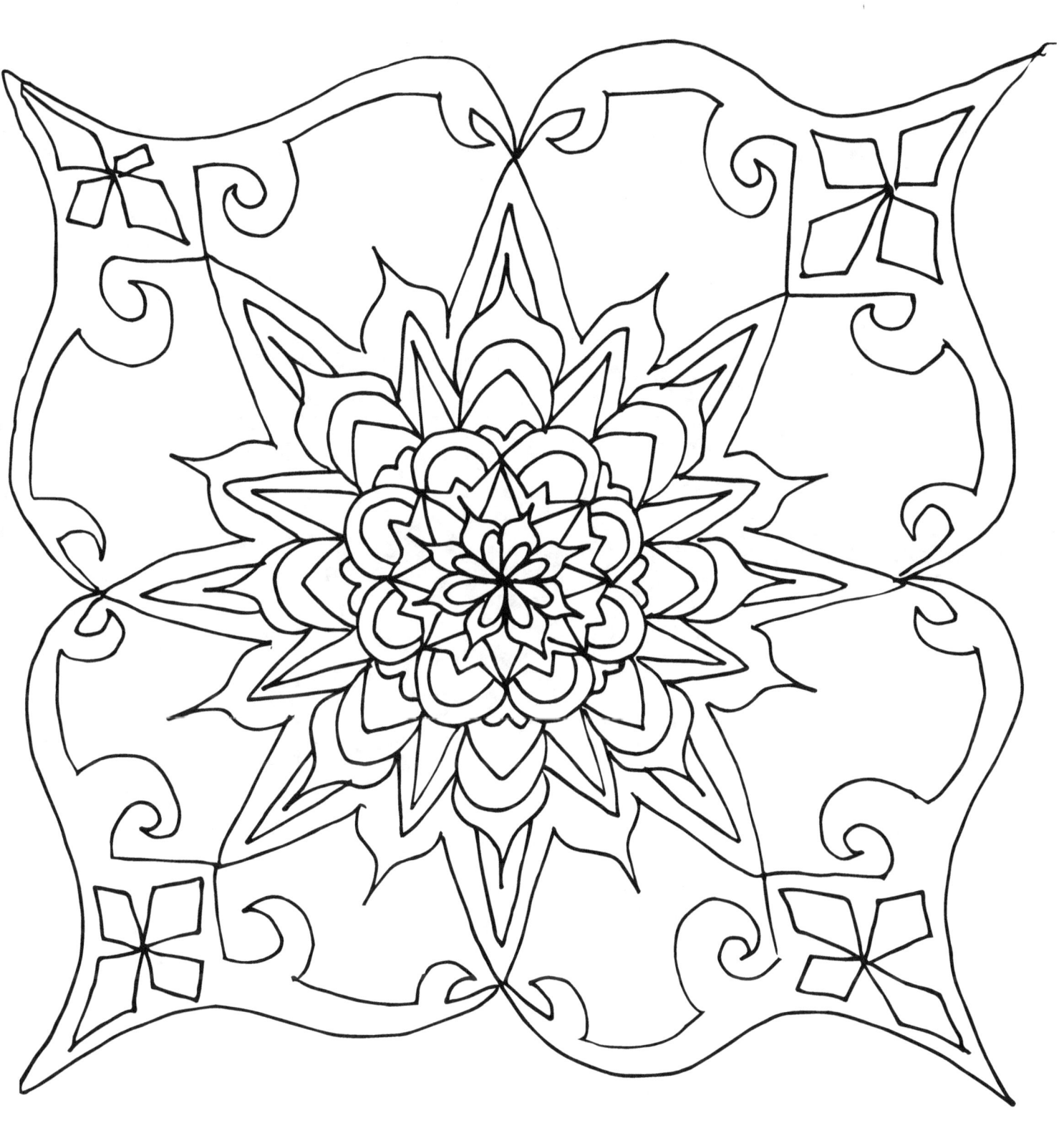

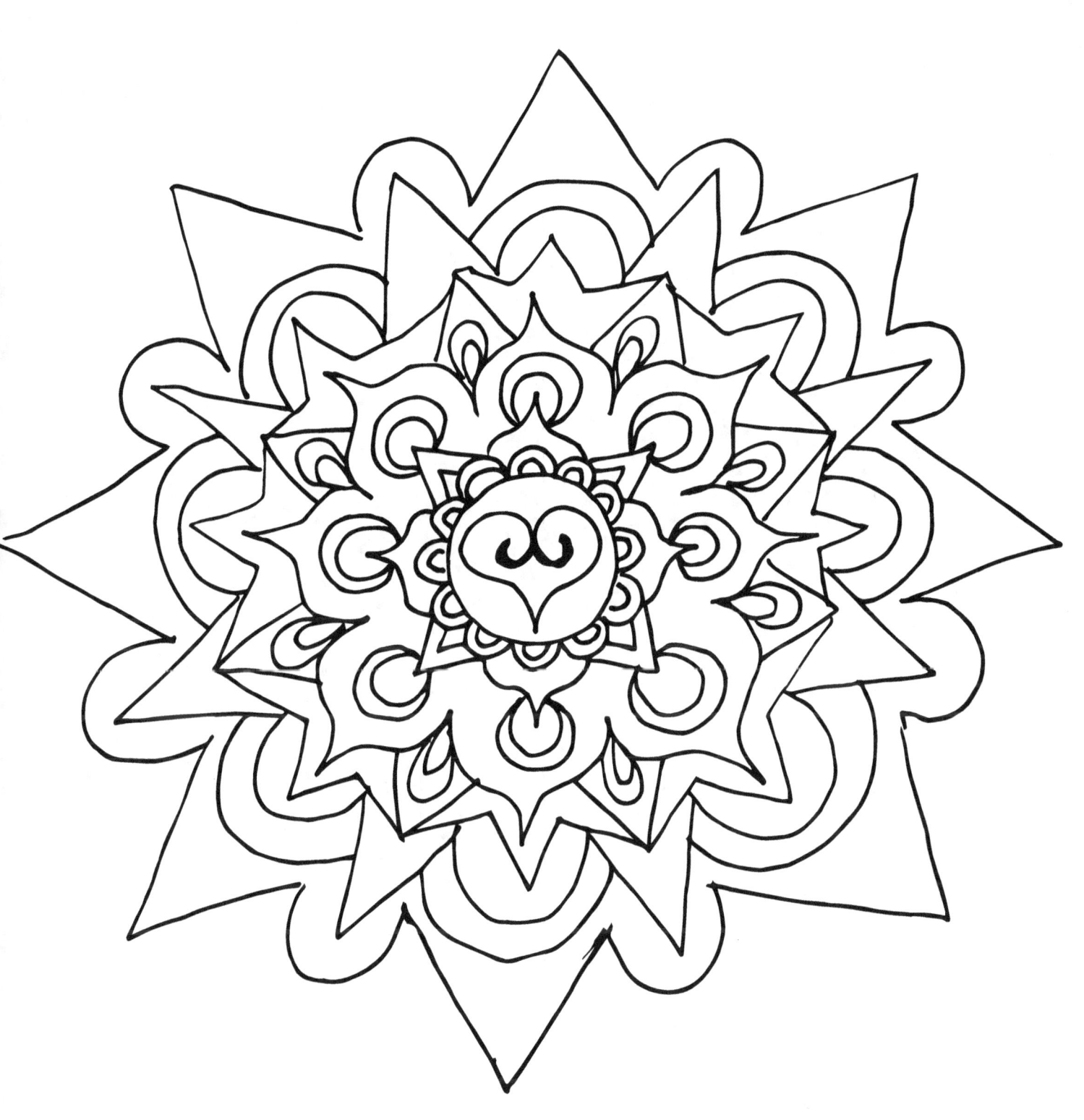

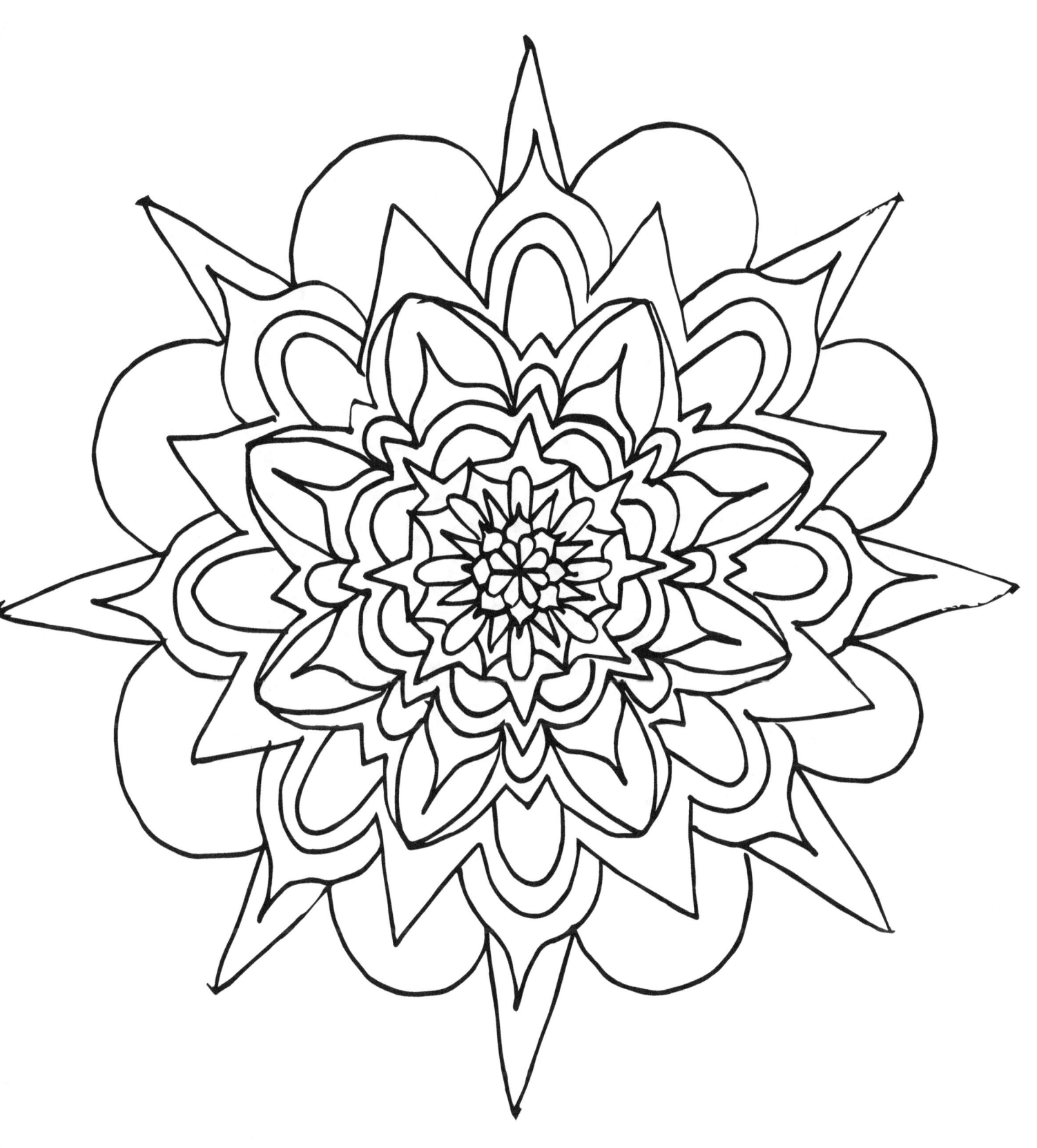

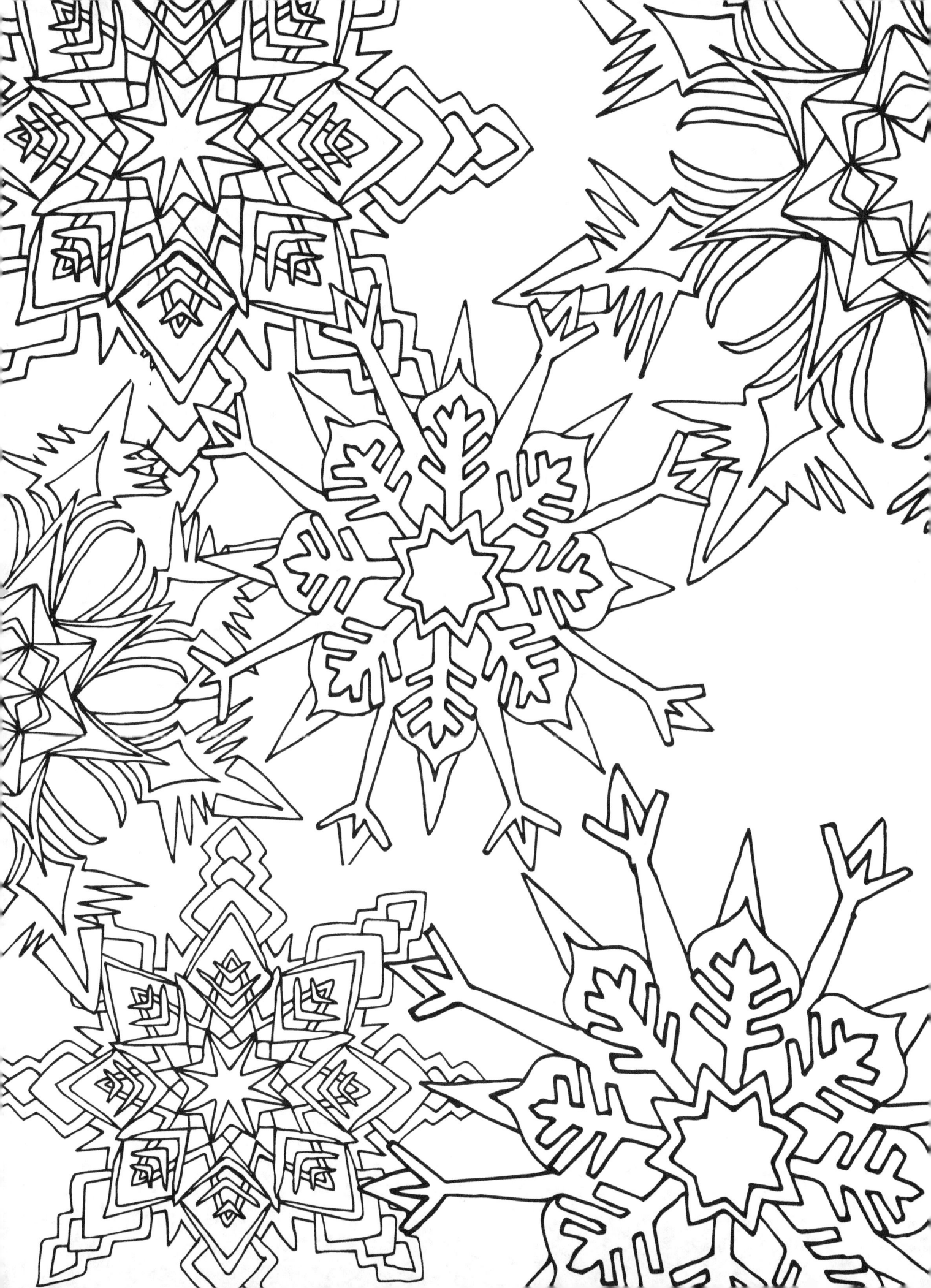

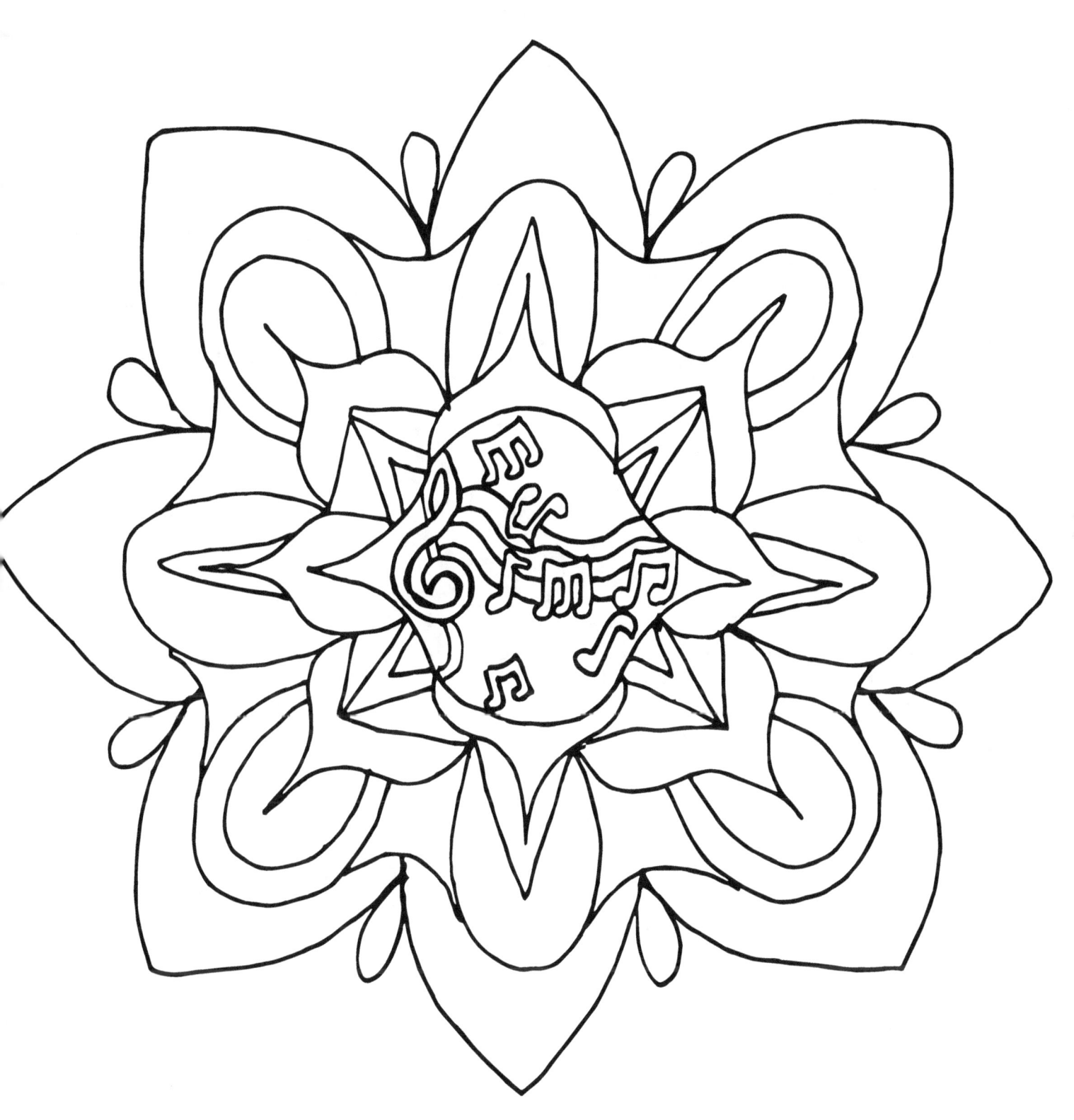

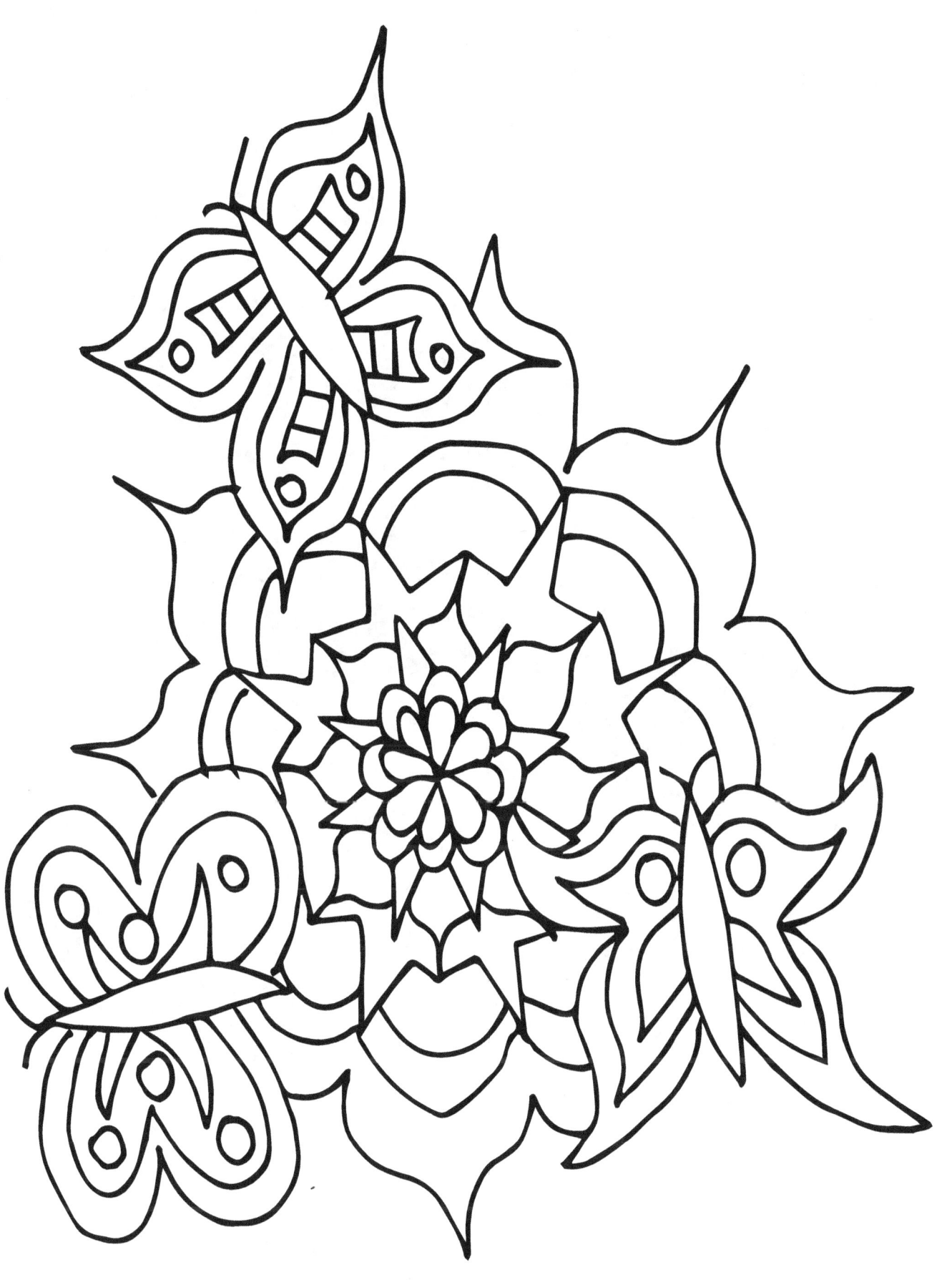

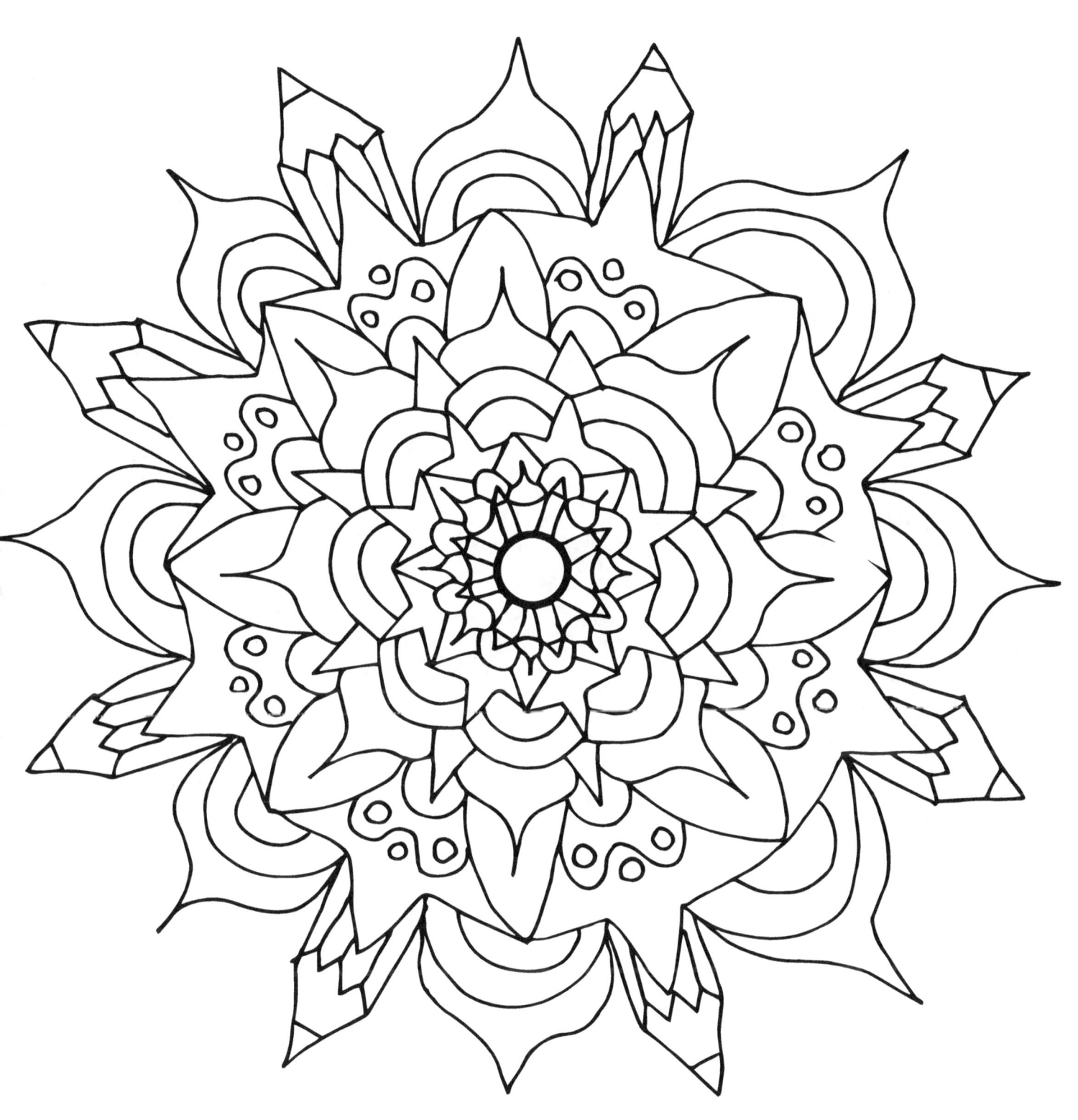

www.ingramcontent.com/pod-product-compliance
Lightning Source LLC
Chambersburg PA
CBHW082347220526
45470CB00008B/2670